International Study Guide

Asian Theology on the Way
Christianity, Culture, and Context

Edited by
Peniel Jesudason Rufus Rajkumar

ASIAN THEOLOGY ON THE WAY

Fortress Press Edition © 2015

Copyright © Peniel Jesudason Rufus Rajkumar 2012. All rights reserved. Except for brief quotations in critical articles or reviews, no part of this book may be reproduced in any manner without prior written permission from the publisher. Visit http://www.augsburgfortress.org/copyrights/ or write to Permissions, Augsburg Fortress, Box 1209, Minneapolis, MN 55440.

Unless otherwise noted, Scripture quotations are taken from the New Revised Standard Version of the Bible, Anglicized Edition, copyright © 1989, 1995 by the Division of Christian Education of the National Council of the Churches of Christ in the USA. Used by permission. All rights reserved.
One extract, marked AV, is from the Authorized Version of the Bible (The King James Bible), the rights in which are vested in the Crown, and is reproduced by permission of the Crown's Patentee, Cambridge University Press.

Cover design: Laurie Ingram

Library of Congress Cataloging-in-Publication Data
Print ISBN: 978-1-4514-9966-7
eBook ISBN: 978-1-5064-0032-7

The paper used in this publication meets the minimum requirements of American National Standard for Information Sciences — Permanence of Paper for Printed Library Materials, ANSI Z329.48-1984.

Manufactured in the U.S.

*Dedicated to the late Professor Arvind P. Nirmal
on the occasion of the thirtieth anniversary of his Carey Society address
at the United Theological College, Bangalore,
which reconfigured the shape of Christian theology
and recharted the course of Indian Christian theology
through the gift of Dalit theology*

Contents

Contributors · vii
The International Study Guides · xi
Acknowledgements · xii
Introduction:
From Asian furrows sprung . . . : Christian theology in Asia
  by Peniel Jesudason Rufus Rajkumar · xiii

Part 1 Asian Christian theology: birds'-eye views of the furrows

1 The task, method and content of Asian theologies · 3
  Sathianathan Clarke

2 Interfaith dialogue and Christian theology in Asia · 14
  Edmund Kee-Fook Chia

3 Asian Christian liberation theology · 23
  Philip Vinod Peacock

4 Cross-textual hermeneutics in Asia · 31
  Archie Chi Chung Lee

Part 2 Fighting foreign fertilizers in the furrows

5 Postcolonial Asian feminist theologies · 41
  Kwok Pui-lan

6 From Orientalism to postcolonial: notes on reading practices · 48
  Rasiah S. Sugirtharajah

7 Postcolonialism and Hong Kong Christianity · 56
  Wai Ching Angela Wong

8 Asian Christologies: a postcolonial reconstruction · 65
  C. I. David Joy

Part 3 New seeds in the furrows

9 Between a rock and a hard place: an Asian theology of survival · 75
  Gemma Tulud Cruz

10	Indigenous theology in Asia: issues and perspectives Wati Longchar	83
11	Pentecostalism in Asia Sunder John Boopalan	97

Part 4 Worms'-eye views of the furrows

12	Minjung theology: whose voice, for whom? Sebastian Kim	111
13	Devious devotion to Christ: the making of Indian Christologies Joseph Prabhakar Dayam	115
14	Contextual Christian theologies in China prior to 1950 Lawrence Braschi	123
15	Dalit theology: the 'untouched' touching theology Peniel Jesudason Rufus Rajkumar	132

Glossary   142
References and further reading   144
Index   155

Contributors

Sunder John Boopalan is currently pursuing his PhD in Religion and Society at Princeton Theological Seminary, Princeton, NJ. His recently published works include 'Exclusion, Experience, Exclusivism and Ecumenism: A. P. Nirmal's Contribution to Indian Christian Theology and its Relevance to Pastoral Ministry', in *Masihi Sevak: Journal of Christian Ministry*, vol. 35, no. 1 (March 2010); and 'Dalit Experience: An Andhra Pradesh Case Study' (co-authored with Joseph Prabhakar Dayam and Peniel Jesudason Rufus Rajkumar) in Kenneth R. Ross, ed., *Edinburgh 2010: Fresh Perspectives on Christian Mission* (2010). Before coming to Princeton he served as a Research Associate with the Collective of Dalit Ecumenical Christian Scholars (CODECS).

Lawrence Braschi is Director of the China Desk at Churches Together in Britain and Ireland and a doctoral student at the School of Oriental and African Studies, London. He has written on the relationship between missionary and government-run education in forming national identity in western China during the early twentieth century, the mass movements among the Miao and Lisu to Christianity, and the place of religion in contemporary China. He is also executive editor of the *China Study Journal*, which publishes translations of contemporary Chinese theological, academic and religious material.

Edmund Kee-Fook Chia joined the Theology Faculty of the Australian Catholic University in Melbourne in July 2011. Previously he was Associate Professor and Chair of the Doctrinal Studies department at the Catholic Theological Union, Chicago. He is editor of *Dialogue? Resource Manual for Catholics in Asia* (2001), and co-editor of *A Longing for Peace: The Challenge of a Multicultural, Multireligious World* (2006) and *Mission After Christendom: Emergent Themes in Contemporary Mission* (2010). He is originally from Malaysia and served as executive secretary of Ecumenical and Interreligious Dialogue for the Catholic Asian Bishops' Conferences from 1996 to 2004. As a systematic theologian he engages in theology from an intercultural and interreligious perspective.

Sathianathan Clarke is Bishop Sundo Kim Chair in World Christianity and Professor of Theology, Culture and Mission, at Wesley Theological Seminary, Washington, DC, USA. For several years (1996–2004) he served as faculty in the Theology and Ethics department at the United Theological College, Bangalore, India. He is the author of *Dalits and Christianity: Subaltern Religion and Liberation Theology in India* (1998) and, with Rowena Robinson, *Religious Conversion in India: Modes, Motivations, Meanings* (2003). More recently he co-edited with Manchala Deenabandhu and Philip Peacock *Dalit Theology in the Twenty-first Century: Discordant Voices, Discerning Pathways* (2010). He is presently working on his forthcoming book, entitled *Competing Religious Fundamentalisms: Twenty-first Century Challenge for Christian Theology*. Dr Clarke is a member of the Archbishop's Commission for Theological Education for the Anglican Communion (TEAC) and the House of Bishops Theological Commission of the Episcopal Church. He was a member of the Bible Study Group that was responsible for designing, preparing and coordinating the Bible studies for Lambeth 2008.

Gemma Tulud Cruz joined the Theology Faculty of the Australian Catholic University in Melbourne in July 2011. She was Assistant Professor of Theology at St Ambrose University, Iowa for two years before moving to Chicago, where she taught in the Catholic Studies department and served as a fellow at the Center for World Catholicism and Intercultural Theology at DePaul University. She is author of *An Intercultural Theology of Migration: Pilgrims in the Wilderness* (2010) and articles on topics such as mission, interreligious dialogue, feminist ethics, and the intersections of theology and culture. She specializes in Feminist Liberation Ethics and Migration Theology and, in addition to presenting papers, has served as consultant at various conferences in Asia, Europe, Australia and North America.

Joseph Prabhakar Dayam is an ordained minister of the Andhra Evangelical Lutheran Church. He is Associate Professor of Christian Theology at the United Theological College, Bangalore. His publications include *Mission At and From the Margins: Patterns, Protagonists and Perspectives* (co-edited with Peniel Jesudason Rufus Rajkumar, forthcoming). He is also the convener of the Collective of Dalit Ecumenical Christian Scholars (CODECS).

C. I. David Joy is a presbyter of the Church of South India, South Kerala Diocese. At present he is a Professor of New Testament at the United Theological College, Bangalore. He is an executive committee member of the Society for Biblical Studies in India and an editor for the *International Journal of Sociology and Anthropology*. His recent books include *Christology Revisited: Profiles and Prospects* (2007), *Mark and its Subalterns: A Hermeneutical Paradigm for a Postcolonial Context* (2008), *Not by the Might but by the Spirit* (2008), and *Kurisile Rithubhedangal* (2009).

Sebastian Kim holds the Chair in Theology and Public Life in the Faculty of Education and Theology at York St John University. Before coming to York, he taught World Christianity and was Director of the Christianity in Asia

Project at the Faculty of Divinity of the University of Cambridge. Before that, he taught at the Cambridge Theological Federation, Cambridge, the Presbyterian College and Theological Seminary, Seoul, and the Union Biblical Seminary, Pune, India. He received his PhD from the Faculty of Divinity, University of Cambridge, and is a Fellow of the Royal Asiatic Society. He is also the editor of the *International Journal of Public Theology*. His recent publications include *Christianity as a World Religion* (co-edited with Kirsteen Kim, 2008) and, as editor, *Christian Theology in Asia* (2008).

Kwok Pui-lan was born in Hong Kong and is William F. Cole Professor of Christian Theology and Spirituality at the Episcopal Divinity School, Cambridge, Massachusetts. Her publications include *Postcolonial Imagination and Feminist Theology* (2005), *Introducing Asian Feminist Theology* (2000) and *Discovering the Bible in the Non-Biblical World* (1995). She is the co-editor of *Off the Menu: Asian and Asian North American Women's Religion and Theology* (2007), and editor of *Hope Abundant: Third World and Indigenous Women's Theology* (2010) and *Women and Christianity* (2010). In 2011 she was President of the American Academy of Religion.

Archie Chi Chung Lee received his doctoral degree in Hebrew Bible Studies at the University of Edinburgh in 1980, having done graduate research work on the Hebrew language and archaeology at the Hebrew University of Jerusalem. He is familiar with the religious, social and political complexity of Israel–Palestine issues and the war with Iraq. From 1998 to 2001 he was the founding director of the Christianity in Asia Project of the Centre for Advanced Religious and Theological Studies, University of Cambridge. His area of specialization is the Hebrew Bible and its socio-political and religio-cultural contexts in Ancient Mesopotamia and Canaan. In recent years he has developed interests in cross-textual hermeneutics, comparative scriptural studies and Asian biblical interpretation. He serves as associate editor or reviewer for four international academic publications: *Global Bible Commentary*, *Cambridge Dictionary of Christianity*, *Journal of Biblical Literature* and *Journal of World Christianity*.

Wati Longchar is an ordained minister from Nagaland. Currently he is Dean of the Doctor of Ministry and Extension Programme of the Senate of Serampore College, West Bengal, India. He is also Director-in-charge of Research at the South Asia Theological and Research Institute, Bangalore. In 2010 he edited *Embracing Enclusive Community: Disability Perspective, Issues in Theological Research: A Methodological Exploration*, and *Edinburgh 2010: Witnessing to Christ Today in India*. He is the editor of *Asia Journal of Theology* and *Journal of Theology and Culture in Asia*.

Philip Vinod Peacock is Associate Professor of Theology and Social Analysis at Bishop's College, Kolkata. His publications include *Dalit Theology in* *the Twenty-First Century: Discordant Voices Discerning Pathways* (co-edited with Sathianathan Clarke and Deenabandhu Manchala, 2010) and *Created in God's Image: From Hegemony to Partnership – A Church Manual on Men as Partners: Promoting Positive Masculinities* (co-edited with Patricia Sheerattan-Bisnauth, 2010).

Peniel Jesudason Rufus Rajkumar is a priest of the Church of South India and teaches Christian Social Ethics at the United Theological College, Bangalore. He is the author of *Challenges of Transition: Religion and Ethics in Changing Contexts* (2007) and *Dalit Theology and Dalit Liberation: Problems, Paradigms and Possibilities* (2010). He is currently co-editing, with Emma Wild-Wood, *Foundations of Mission*, a book project commissioned by the Edinburgh 2010 Study Process Monitoring Group. Before coming to India he served as an assistant curate in the Diocese of London.

Rasiah S. Sugirtharajah is Professor of Biblical Hermeneutics at the University of Birmingham. His most recent publications include (as editor) *Caught Reading Again: Scholars and Their Books* (2009), and *Troublesome Texts: The Bible in Colonial and Contemporary Culture* (2008). He has written and edited several books on postcolonial biblical interpretation. Earlier he served as Lecturer in Third World Theologies at Selly Oak Colleges, and was on the staff of Tamil Nadu Theological Seminary, Madurai and Serampore College.

Wai Ching Angela Wong is Associate Professor of the Department of Cultural and Religious Studies in the Chinese University of Hong Kong. She is also Head of the Graduate Division of Gender Studies and Co-Director of the Gender Research Centre at the same university. Her publications include *'The Poor Woman': A Critical Analysis of Asian Theology and Contemporary Chinese Fiction by Women* (2002), 'Negotiating Gender: Postcolonialism and Hong Kong Christian Women', in *Gender and Society in Hong Kong* (2003), 'Our Stories Our Bodies: Narrating Female Sexuality in Hong Kong', in *Mainstreaming Gender in Hong Kong Society* (2009), and *Chinese Women and Hong Kong Christianity: An Oral History* (co-edited with Choi Poking, 2010).

The International Study Guides

The global nature of Christianity has become perhaps its most defining feature in the last century. The need for resources that reflect this nature not only in topic but in approach and authorship has never been greater. To meet this need Fortress Press is proud to present a curated selection of volumes from the International Study Guides series. The product of a decades-long commitment on the part of the Society for Promoting Christian Knowledge (SPCK), the International Study Guides present projects in Bible, theology, and Christian history from a decidedly global vantage point.

Acknowledgements

This book owes its existence to the support of several friends. A great debt is due to Dr Emma Wild-Wood, former Commissioning Editor of the SPCK International Study Guides series, who has been a reservoir of patience and encouragement throughout. She has brought perspective to the manuscript through her careful, erudite and perceptive interventions, and I have learnt a great deal from her editorial suggestions and critical comments. I am thankful to David Craig, manager of SPCK Worldwide, who has patiently ensured that the project is completed, and to Lauren Zimmerman, assistant editor at SPCK, for her effective administrative support. The care and enthusiasm that they have invested in the production of this book is greatly appreciated. I am also greatly indebted to Dr Rima Devereaux and Steve Gove for the meticulous attention they have paid towards the preparation of this book.

Sincere gratitude is also due to Prof. R. S. Sugirtharajah and to Prof. Sebastian C. Kim, who generously gave me permission to reproduce earlier articles written by them as part of this volume, and to the Revd Dr Wati Longchar (Interim Director of SATHRI, Bangalore and manager of the *Asia Journal of Theology*) and the Revd Dr Ashish Amos of ISPCK, New Delhi, who, as the respective publishers, facilitated the smooth passage of these reproductions. I am deeply grateful to the individual authors of this volume who have willingly participated in the project by writing new articles and have so generously contributed their time, thoughts and efforts despite their gruelling schedules as busy academics.

My family has been a source of strength for me throughout this project and I am particularly grateful to my parents, Banaya Thrilok Rajkumar and Mrs Kiruba Rajkumar, for selflessly helping me with childcare during the early stages of this project, when my wife Rebecca was completing her studies in London. Finally, my wife Rebecca and son Ebenezer have, through the course of this project, never failed to surprise me with their love and sustain me with their understanding, even as they wondered whether and when this project would come to an end. The fact that it did owes a lot to them.

Introduction
From Asian furrows sprung . . . : Christian theology in Asia

Peniel Jesudason Rufus Rajkumar

With the shift in the gravity of world Christianity towards the 'Global South', the needle of the compass of Christian theology can no longer be oriented towards the North. In such a context there is an urgent need to revisit Christian theology from a Southern perspective. If the distinction between Global North and Global South is taken seriously, this reader might be seen to belong to a series of theological books focusing on 'Theology Facing Southwards'. It is designed to replace *A Reader in Indian Christian Theology*, edited by Cecil Hargreaves and R. S. Sugirtharajah, and, following Diane Stinton's reader in African theology, titled *African Theology on the Way: Current Conversations*, revisits the various paths that Christian theology has trodden in Asia.

However, rather than retreading the paths of Asian theology, this reader is more about *following the furrows*. It is about theology sprung from the furrows of Asia. But why an agricultural metaphor? And why the metaphor of 'furrows'? A simple answer is that Asia is a predominantly agricultural continent where furrows are a familiar sight. Asian Christian theologians have always playfully engaged with agricultural metaphors and therefore the present attempt can be understood as falling in line with that tradition. The Japanese theologian Kosuke Koyama writes of theology as 'an exciting report on our having rice with Jesus' (Koyama, 1972: 19). Agriculture sustains the livelihood and lives of countless Asians, many of whom have rice as their staple food. Therefore the use of an agricultural metaphor should be understood as an attempt to interpret Asian Christian theology as a theology of life which is both life-giving and life-sustaining.

In introducing Asian Christian theology, however, there are several other reasons why I chose the agricultural metaphor of furrows. The image of furrows in my opinion captures one defining characteristic of Asian Christian theology – that it is *embedded in* and *emerges from* its context. The metaphor captures the element of 'contextuality'. Of course all theology is contextual, but in some contexts the theological task involves less toil and struggle and

Introduction

is less connected to the dirt and soil of life's earthliness. The metaphor of the furrows captures the hard work, the patient waiting and the potential risks that are involved in bringing something like Asian Christian theologies to life. The metaphor of the furrow from which new life sprouts resonates with another metaphor – the metaphor of the womb – which is also a source of new life. C. S. Song has already written about 'Theology from the Womb of Asia'. The metaphor of the furrow is chosen to convey this idea – of a theology birthed from the eclectic Asian context. The furrow is a metaphor which can hold within its embrace concepts which have often been used in connection with theologizing in the Asian context, such as 'theology from the grassroots' and 'theology from the dusty soil' by Wilfred.

The furrow is not only an agricultural metaphor, it also has theological connotations. We find references to furrows in the book of Psalms. I would like to highlight two uses of the metaphor in the Psalms. The first reference comes in Psalm 65.10 where God is portrayed as the one who waters the earth's furrows abundantly, settles its ridges, softens it with showers and blesses its growth. The metaphor of the furrows has also been chosen, therefore, because this volume not only seeks to celebrate the abundant growth of Christian theologies in Asia but also to emphasize that the story of the shoots of Christian theology flourishing in the Asian context is the story of God's gentle tending of the soil – of God's watering and weeding, nurturing the seedlings as they take root and spring forth to life.

The metaphor occurs again in the Psalms, although in a different context. In Psalm 129.3 it is used by the Psalmist as a metaphor of affliction: 'Those who plough ploughed on my back; they made their furrows long.' The use of the metaphor here connotes pain and distress. It is a poignant reminder of the various struggles for life and dignity that have taken place in Asia. Christian theology in Asia has been 'marked' by such furrows on its back, especially in the case of Minjung theology in Korea, Burakhumin theology in Japan and Dalit theology in India. It is in the midst of these struggles – the furrows that hurt sharply and deeply – that Asian Christian theology was born.

This volume is in one way a 'theo-story' – the story of God finding and making a home in Asia. It is also a 'peoples-story' – of how Asian Christians have discerned God's presence and decried God's seeming absence in their own (hi)stories, of how they have related God and represented Jesus Christ to their neighbours of different faiths and of how they have sought to foster avenues for peace and forge visions of justice as part of their faith-commitment to follow Christ. As you read the accounts of theology presented here, ask yourself which approaches come closest to how you discern God's presence and how you relate to Jesus Christ in your own context. And then ask why that is.

Returning to the central metaphor of this volume, a furrow is made by a plough which is drawn by a pair of oxen yoked together. The story of Christian theology in Asia has been a story of its yoking with Asia's cultures and religious traditions. Christian thought has been co-yoked with

Introduction

aspects of Asian culture and religiosity; the Bible has been co-yoked with other religious texts and oral traditions in order to prepare the furrows from which enriching and edifying theological discourses have sprouted to life. Christian theology in Asia has often been a conversation between the co-yoked. Do you have aspects of culture and tradition that are yoked to your Christian thought in your own context? Do you see such yoking as helpful or unhelpful for understanding God's work in the world? Why do you make this assessment?

The intention of this volume is to introduce its readers to the conversational, the concrete and the contextual dimensions of Asian Christian theology, by which is meant Christian theology in the diverse Asian contexts. As a theology which has undertaken the 'Double Baptism' of which Aloysius Pieris speaks – the baptism in the Jordan of Asia's multi-religiousness and the Calvary of Asia's poverty – Christian theology in Asia has on the one hand conversed with the continent's diverse cultures as well as its multi-religiosity and on the other critically and constructively engaged with the challenges posed by its various social, economic and political contexts. Thus, Asian Christian theology has been necessarily concrete, contextual and conversational.

In its attempt to re-present the narrative of Jesus, the journeying Christ, finding a home within Asian thought and amid the paradoxical reality of Asian life, the essays in this volume are categorized in four parts. Part 1 gives us a broad overview of Christian theology in the Asian context. Like birds eyeing the furrows from a distance, the views in this section are broad and comprehensive in terms of what they cover and focus on different aspects of Asian Christian theology. The first chapter, by Sathianathan Clarke, is introductory in nature. It sets the scene by discussing three important themes of Asian Christian theology, namely solidarity with neighbours of differing religious faiths; hope for the poor and marginalized; and Asian biblical interpretation in the multi-scriptural and postcolonial context of Asia. These themes are discussed in the three chapters which follow, by Chia, Peacock and Lee.

Part 2 introduces us to the influence of postcolonialism on Christianity and Christian theologizing in Asia. The furrows of Asian Christianity have undergone phases where harmful foreign fertilizers have been used 'for the flourishing' of Christianity and Christian theology and to get rid of the 'pests' of native culture, customs and practices. The four chapters in this section by Kwok, Sugirtharajah, Wong and Joy highlight how Christianity and Christian theology have engaged with the challenges posed by the legacy of colonialism which permeates Asian Christianity and is an inescapable reality in Asia. 'From Orientalism to post-colonial: notes on reading practices' by R. S. Sugirtharajah, originally published in the *Asia Journal of Theology*, vol. 10, no. 1, pp. 20–7, is reproduced here with the kind permission of the author and publisher.

Part 3 focuses on themes and trends in Asian theology which have not been adequately represented in general introductions to Asian Christian theology and have remained 'specialist concerns'. While Gemma Tulud Cruz introduces us to how marginal groups in Asia skilfully forge their survival amid everyday struggles and suffering, Wati Longchar brings out the distinctive features of indigenous theologies which are counter-intuitive to the contemporary notions of growth and development in a globalized world that pose threats to indigenous ways of life. Sunder John Boopalan complements the other two essays in this section by bringing out the multi-faceted dimensions of Pentecostalism in Asia, which has experienced exponential growth in recent years. Since these are themes which many new readers of Asian Christian theology will not be familiar with, the space allotted for these three articles is relatively generous.

Part 4 gives us glimpses of certain modes of contextual theologizing in Asia. I am indebted to John Boopalan for the idea of the 'worms'-eye view', which I borrow here. Of the four essays which comprise this section, 'Minjung theology: whose voice, for whom?' by Sebastian Kim earlier appeared in Israel Selvanayagam (ed.), *Moving Forms of Theology: Faith Talk's Changing Contexts* (New Delhi: ISPCK, 2002) and is reproduced here with the kind permission of the author and publisher. I am aware that this section could have been more exhaustive. For instance, given the fact that Philippines is probably the only Asian country where Christianity is the predominant religion, a chapter on Filipino contextual theology (which was originally planned) would have been appropriate. A focus on Christian theologizing in countries like Vietnam, Burma, Indonesia and Malaysia could have greatly enhanced the comprehensiveness of this reader. The incompleteness of this selection is embraced in the hope of completion in the future. The worms'-eye views in this section by Kim, Dayam, Braschi and Rajkumar are focused on specific contexts and are, so to speak, 'closer to the ground'.

The four parts of this volume seek to capture the various modes of *doing* and *living* theology in Asia. Not only do they draw our attention to the different furrows from which Asian Christian theologies have emerged; in the process they also introduce us to the forces which have, like the oxen carrying the yoke of the plough, given shape to the furrows of Asian theology. They also introduce us to the several *agents* who, like the earthworms in the soil, have not only enhanced the fertility of the furrows of Asian Christian theology but also offer, despite their threatened existence, visible signs of life, bearing testimony that Asian Christian theologies are living and life-enhancing theologies. It is to this testimony of life – the fruits of the furrows – that this volume seeks to bear witness.

Friends, this book is intended not simply to extend your knowledge about Asian theologies. It is also intended to provide you with some tools with which to do your own theologizing. As you read the book, think about how each chapter might help you in your own thinking about God and action with God in your own context. The intention of this volume is to prompt both thinking and discussion on living out the Christian faith in context.

Therefore, in some ways it is an invitation to each one of us to become worms ourselves – worms which are relentlessly and tirelessly involved in fertilizing the soil of faith and which, despite the risks, are engaged in maintaining a resolute and resilient presence which bears witness to the life-giving dimensions of Christ's gospel of life in all its fullness.

Part 1
Asian Christian theology: birds'-eye views of the furrows

1
The task, method and content of Asian theologies

Sathianathan Clarke

 Abstract

In this chapter Clarke identifies five defining dimensions of theologizing in Asia. He characterizes Asian Christian theology as human reflection on a shared God and Christian reflection on Jesus as the interpreter of God and human beings; as a communitarian theology; as a discerning and critical theology; as a constructive theology; and as a transformational theology which pursues life in all its fullness. He further explores three significant themes that represent the content of Asian Christian theology: building solidarity with neighbours of different faiths through widening the understanding of God; constructing a historically concrete Jesus who gives voice to the cries and lifts up the hope of Asia's poor and marginalized; and developing complementary modes of biblical interpretation in response to the multi-scriptural and postcolonial Asian context.

 Introduction

Although constructed as a single entity, the continent of Asia contains a multitude of realities. From one viewpoint an essentially united world-view lies at the heart of these complex and various interpretations of reality. This vision is well articulated by Okakura Kakuzo in the opening lines of his book *The Ideals of the East*:

> Asia is one. The Himalayas divide, only to accentuate, two mighty civilizations, the Chinese with its communism of Confucius, and the Indian with its individualism of Vedas. But not even the snowy barriers can interrupt for one moment that broad expanse of love for the Ultimate and the Universal, which is the common thought-inheritance of every Asiatic race . . .
>
> (Kakuzo, 1903: 1)

Quite contrary to this unitary conception of Asia exists another, pluralistic version. Different peoples with unique histories, world-views, ethnicities and national aspirations appear to be forced into a common mould under the gaze of colonialism. Leo Ching, in reaction to views such as those of Kakuzo, states:

> Asia is neither a cultural, religious or linguistic unity nor a unified world. The principle of its unity lies outside of itself, in relation to (an)Other. If one can ascribe to Asia any vague sense of unity, it is that which is excluded and objectified by the west in service of its historical progress. Asia is, and can be one, only under the imperial eye of the west.   (Ching, 1988)

It is within the contrast between this oneness and these pluralities that Asian theology/ies must be located. Of course, this discourse is itself projected as a unitary phenomenon; and yet it is articulated by many communities, contexts and histories. Having admitted to this apparent paradox, I shall for reasons of style and simplicity refer to the area of theological reflection that I shall explore in this chapter as 'Asian theology'.

This essay has two parts. In the first part, which deals with the formal side of the discipline, I offer a definition of Asian Christian theology and then explicate some of its methodological features. In the second part, which represents the material side, I examine three substantial theological themes that have taken centre stage in Asia.

A definition of Asian theology: its method and task

I shall begin expounding the task and method of Asian theology by offering a definition. Asian Christian theology, I suggest, is collective reflection on God, the world and human beings and their interrelationships, this reflection being framed by Jesus Christ and formed through the Holy Spirit in light of the realities of the peoples of Asia for the purpose of transforming the life of the world in accordance with the good news that 'the kingdom of God is at hand' (Mark 1.15). Let me elucidate this dense definition by exploring five elements that capture the various dimensions of theology in Asia.

First, Asian Christian theology is human reflection on a shared God and Christian reflection on Jesus Christ as the interpreter of God and human beings. Asian theology is not mere reporting or announcing of pre-packaged knowledge from God. It is human reflection on what is affirmed to be divinely inspired knowledge of God. It is reflection by human beings for their fullness of life in harmony with the rest of creation for the purpose of bringing glory to God. A commonality with other religious communities is readily accepted in Asia, and celebrates our common human flourishing that glorifies God our universal and shared creator. Yet the distinctiveness of Asian Christian theology comes from a prior commitment that lifts up Jesus Christ as *the exact image of God* and *the complete image of human beings* to frame this reflection. The power of the Holy Spirit guides both the commonality (God as universal Creator) and the particularity (Jesus Christ as concrete mediator) of such reflection into ever new truth.

Second, Asian Christian theology is communitarian. Asian theology is personal but not private. Both in its reception by the community of the faithful and in its faithful expression in Church and society, theology interacts with other voices, beliefs and experiences. A sense of humility is built into the vocation of Asian theologians. Despite the spread of the contemporary globalized ethos of individualism and egotism, the idea that theology only pertains to me and 'my sweet Lord' is untenable in Asia. Nor is the practice of Asian theology relegated to deeply inspired Eastern mystics and brilliantly trained oriental academics. The democratization of Asian theology and the consequent interruptions by those seeking to engage in dialogue may generate a more messy and thus less neatly packaged theology, but they help to bring to theological activity the questions and the answers of all God's people. Asian theologians are called to exercise patience. Their work needs to be carried out in conversation with the broader vision of the community and more subaltern versions of theologies of the people. This commitment to include ordinary people in theological reflection is an important aspect of Asian theology.

These first two characteristics of Asian theology are well articulated by Kwok-keung Yeung:

> First, theologians should turn their eyes away from the play of abstract ideas and theologize instead with the living cultures of ordinary people. Second, no single theology could claim universality or exercise dominance over other cultures. [Thus,] Asian theologians have concluded that theologies should be living and plural. (Yeung, 2002: 152)

Third, Asian Christian theology is not uncritically absorptive. When we characterize theology as critical, we must be conscious that we thereby imply two different meanings. The first meaning has to do with the fact that theology deals with important, indeed crucial matters. Sometimes we overlook the fact that critical means extremely important (i.e. 'This procedure is critical to saving the life of this woman' or 'The critical part of the plot can be found only in the dreadfully dull tenth chapter of this long book'). The importance of theology stems from the fact that it always seeks to be accountable to God as well as to people. However, we cannot shy away from a second aspect of our theological activity, which entails the discriminating faculty of reason. This is the more popular use of the term 'critical'. It is also the most distrusted, but a qualification may make it more appealing. It may help in the Asian context to use the terms 'discerning' or 'reflective' to express this critical function that has been gifted by God to human beings. Human beings, as distinct from other living organisms, have the ability to be reflective both about themselves and about their context. These dimensions of being discerning are intrinsic to Asian theology.

Fourth, there is a constructive element to Asian Christian theology. Human beings live within the gifts of inherited traditions and the constructs of imagined futures. 'No one puts new wine into old wineskins; otherwise the new wine will burst the skins and will be spilled, and the skins will be destroyed. But the new wine must be put into fresh wineskins' (Luke 5.37, 38). In this sense Asian Christian theology is not cyclical or circular. It does not seek to come back to the same starting point. It, so to speak, 'reinvents the wheel' in order to spin new historical paths and diverse human patterns. The non-cyclical movement of God in history leads to new forms of the present, which in turn disrupts and frees the future from inherited cyclical patterns of history and fixed notions of God's will. In Asia this infusing of the imaginative and creative has helped in rescuing theology from academic pundits and priestly narrators, and in incorporating in their place the work of artists and prophets.

Finally, transformative objectives of life in all its wholeness permeate Asian Christian theology. Asian theology is not only 'discourse or words about God'. It is also about changing the course of the dis-ease that undermines life as God desires it for all of creation. It persuades the realities of the world and human beings to fit into God's gift of the 'kingdom of God'. Tissa Balasuriya's notion of 'planetary theology' accordingly presents an idea of liberation that encompasses a harmonious order integrating all aspects of life: the individual, societies, cultures, religions and various elements of the cosmos (Balasuriya, 1984). For more than half a century Raimon Panikkar has insisted that such a restored reality is always 'cosmotheandric' (where *cosmos*, cosmic order, *theos*, the divine, and *anthropos*, the human, are reconciled into 'The Rhythm of Being'). Joseph Prabhu's Foreword to Panikkar's recent magnum opus puts this succinctly: for Panikkar, 'the Triadic structure of Reality comprises the Divine, the Human and the Cosmic in thoroughgoing relationality' (Prabhu, 2010: xvii).

Theology thus cannot be about transformation of any of these components of reality in isolation.

> Asian Christian theology is concerned with mending the relationship between God, the world and human beings, because the vision of God for all creation (the Christian gospel's central proclamation identifies this with the 'kingdom of God') lies in their just and proper alignment.

Three themes that represent the content of Asian theology

Keeping these formal features in the background, I shall now examine a selection of themes that reflect the content of theology as expressed in the Asian continent. Clearly all such bundling of motifs reflects the particular perspectives and special commitments of whoever selects the material and explicates the subject matter. The bias toward choosing, circulating and advocating liberational, contextual, constructive, and unconventional trajectories in theologizing is explicitly acknowledged. As I interpret the content of Asian theology in the twenty-first century, I identify three broad themes that have gained a significant foothold.

Religious pluralism in Asian theology

First, theologizing in Asia has sought to forge solidarity between Christians and their neighbours of differing religious faiths by creating spaciousness in God.

> Religious pluralism is at the heart of Asian empirical reality. It fills every geographic nook and cranny of her soils and waters.

Through history these waters have overflowed into every region of the world. Thus, west Asia gave birth to Judaism, Christianity and Islam; south Asia spawned (or generated) Hinduism, Buddhism, Jainism and Sikhism; and east Asia engendered Confucianism, Taoism, Shinto and Shamanism. In this sea of living religions, Christianity is a small watering hole. Whatever statistics one draws upon there appears to be agreement that Christians made up less than ten per cent of the population of Asia in 2010. Asian Christians have often found themselves theologically estranged from the majority of their neighbours, who lived happily within commitment to other religious traditions. This historical circumstance has obliged them to work towards a theology that is at once both passionately Christian and respectfully interreligious. It has been impossible to maintain an imperialistic view of other religions within the bounds of such intimate community. The way in which Asian theologians explicate their faith and practice is marked by the fact that their religion exists in a continent that is more than 90 per cent non-Christian. R. S. Sugirtharajah expresses the positive side of this awareness:

> The basic thrust now is not the declaration of the gospel in an Asian style but discerning it afresh in the ongoing broken relationships between different communities and between human communities and the created order. The task is seen not as adapting the Christian gospel in Asian idioms but

as reconceptualizing the basic tenets of the Christian faith in the light of Asian realities. (Sugirtharajah, 1994: 5)

Trust has therefore arisen in the *spaciousness* of God, stirring theology in Asia to embrace other religious experiences and traditions. The abundance within God is reclaimed graciously and generously in order to re-member and re-integrate local and native cultural and religious experiences and traditions, and thus to reclaim the identity of Asian communities that were fragmented or overpowered by colonial forms of Christianity. This divine capaciousness (largeness) frees Asian Christian communities to grant theological value to the divine experiences that nourished their lives before they accepted Jesus as Lord. This emphasis on God's spaciousness also permits Asian theologians working in religiously plural settings to retain, utilize and celebrate the religious and cultural resources available to their non-Christian families, neighbours and ancestors. Stanley Samartha is an early voice who cogently worked on de-parochializing (undoing the narrowness of) God:

> A process of rejecting exclusive claims and seeking new ways of understanding the relationship of Jesus Christ to God and humanity is already underway. From what may be described as 'normative exclusivism,' Christians are moving toward a position of 'relational distinctiveness' of Christ. It is relational because Christ does not remain unrelated to neighbors of other faiths, and distinctive because without recognizing the distinctiveness of the great religious traditions as different responses to the Mystery of God, no mutual enrichment is possible. (Samartha, 1991: 76, 77)

This is also the direction of Japanese theologian Kosuke Koyama's early plea to consider an expansive and interreligious Christology in conversation with Greek and Buddhist religious thought and philosophy. In a chapter entitled 'Aristotelian Pepper and Buddhist Salt' he writes, 'Yet Christ will be a "tasty" Christ not in the outright rejection of both Aristotelian pepper and Buddhist salt, but rather in using them . . . How can one use Aristotle and Buddha (the two great sages) to articulate Jesus Christ biblically in Thailand?' (Koyama, 1974: 287).

Jesus and the poor in Asian theology

Second, making God more capacious does not prevent theology from establishing a historically concrete Jesus who amplifies the cry and lifts high the hope of the Asian poor and marginalized.

In spite of the focus on Africa in most global discourses of 'the bottom billion', Asia in the twenty-first century still has the highest living number of poor people. Ironically this state of affairs has coincided with the rise of China, Korea and India as major global economic powers. Furthermore, the growing disparity between the rich and the poor in Asia is cause for concern. While the shrinking of the world has become a hallmark of life today, economic globalization has not led to a more economically just world order. Amartya Sen is acutely aware of the power imbalances inherent in globalization. But more importantly he identifies the growing number of voices that refuse to accept such a situation in the twenty-first century:

> Indeed, the real debate on globalization is, ultimately, not about the efficiency of the markets, nor about the importance of modern technology. The debate, rather, is about the severe asymmetries of power, for which there is much less tolerance now than in the world that emerged at the end of the Second World War . . . what is absolutely clear is that people are far less willing to accept massive inequalities than they were in 1944 . . .   (Sen, 2005: 342, 343)

Asian theology joins in this critique of globalization from the standpoint of the poor and excluded.

In response to this prevailing situation of poverty, theology in Asia includes in its agenda the plight of the economically and socially marginalized by tapping into the liberative potential of Jesus.

Making space in the abstractions of a universal God (in the Asian multifaith context) needs to be accompanied by putting forward the subversive and liberating dimensions of the historical Jesus (in the Asian context of poverty). Aloysius Pieris consistently talks about this dual Asian context, one which involves 'the many religions and the many poor' (Pieris, 1994: 143).

Asian theology will not allow the historical Jesus to rest in peace and remain withdrawn from the suffering experienced by the poor and by marginalized communities, or from the hope for freedom their cries express. Various regional Christologies have reclaimed Jesus as one of themselves in their struggle against ruthless traditional regimes and ideologies operating in collaboration with profit-driven transnational corporations. Minjung theology from Korea focuses on the working poor, exploited as they are by the nation state in connivance with burgeoning corporations. Dalit and Tribal theologies from India foreground the cry of what were once referred to as the untouchables (they themselves prefer the term 'Dalit', which means 'broken ones') and Tribals (they prefer 'Adivasi', which means 'original dwellers'). Women join this discourse by calling upon Jesus to challenge Asian patriarchy in its historic and modern forms. In many instances, the historical Jesus is promoted as the sole basis and criterion for the role of Asian Christian theology in warding off the defacing and hegemonic consequences of other, dominant theologies. By identifying the solidarity of the historical Jesus with the poor and the excluded, Asian theology gives value to such people's existential situation and connects this with God's mission to free and uplift them. The human Jesus was the Human One from God who identified with and continues to work with the poor, the colonized, Minjung, Dalits, Adivasis, othered women, and the outcast in their right to live as human beings with dignity and justice. C. S. Song powerfully links the historical Jesus to such marginalized groups:

> Jesus, in short, is the crucified people! Jesus means crucified people. To say Jesus is to say suffering people. To know Jesus is to know suffering people. Traditional Christian theology tells us that to know Jesus we must know God first. But we stress that to know God we must know Jesus, because Jesus makes God real to us. Now we must go even farther: to know Jesus we must know people . . . By people I mean those men, women, and children, in Jesus' day, today, and in the days to come, economically exploited, politically oppressed, culturally and religiously alienated, sexually, racially, or class-wise discriminated against.
>
> (Song, 2000: 215, 216)

In focusing on the theological rejection of dominant and powerful models of human social and economic organization, one cannot ignore the forceful and creative contribution of Asian feminists as they make Jesus take on the oppressive, cumulative and all-encompassing system of patriarchy. Etched into centuries of cultural and religious traditions, systems of patriarchal privilege were embedded in the prevalent constructs of gender relations, affecting women both in the Church and in society at large. Asian women have built a powerful movement to challenge the legitimacy of such forms of patriarchy. Let me list two creative offerings that mark this reclamation of Jesus by Asian women.

First, from the Philippines, and in continuity with the work of Virginia Fabella and Mary John Mananzan, who urged a shift in emphasis from the historical accident of Jesus' maleness to the ontological significance of the liberation process that he initiated, Muriel Orevillo-Montenegro makes a notable contribution. She interprets Jesus through 'the many-breasted mother' known in Filipino mythology as *Inang Bayan* (literally 'the mother of the land and people'). Like Inang Bayan, Jesus wept with his people, was slain for them, and yet 'rises again and again in the communities that continue to struggle for fullness of life' (Orevillo-Montenegro, 2006: 198). Second, from a Korean context that draws heavily on shamanistic religion and culture, Chung Hyun Kyung proposes the notion of 'Jesus as Priest of *Han*'. In employing the term *han* (which refers to the intense burdens that build up as a result of oppression and injustice) she identifies a liberative role for Jesus, especially in connection with Asian women. In her words, 'As a Korean shaman has been healer, comforter and counselor for Korean women, Jesus Christ healed and comforted women in his ministry' (Chung, 1990: 66).

Asian theology in a multi-scriptural context

Third, the multi-scriptural context and the postcolonial situation of Asia give rise to quite different yet complementary modes of Bible interpretation in the continent.

Religious fascination and engagement with the Bible has always been part of Asian theology. However, while gratitude and reverence were evident in a multi-religious context, one in which Scripture was a means of preserving and promoting fullness of life, such engagement tended to engender suspicion and scepticism in a postcolonial situation, wherein the Bible had been used as a means of legitimizing and expanding colonialism.

The multi-scriptural context of Asia, on the other hand, has influenced Christian theology to cherish its own textual narrative while also respecting other expressions of sacred wisdom. Thus, reading the Bible alongside the sacred scriptures of Hindus, Muslims and Buddhists opens up genuinely creative spaces for 'reading religious texts interreligiously'. Peter Phan points out the edifying consequences of such intertextual interpretations:

> It is not a matter of choosing light against darkness, truth against error, goodness against evil, beauty against ugliness. Rather, it is more a matter of including and integrating the new insights one has gathered from an interreligious reading of the non-Christian scriptures into a new formulation of the Christian faith and practice. (Phan, 2009: 330)

The significations of the Bible cannot be understood in isolation from the pre-existing world of religious texts that is part of the social memory and practice of Asian communities. The value of the Bible is enhanced rather than diminished within such a historical setting, a fact that takes on special significance among communities that have been denied access to Scripture. As an example, we can cite the reception and valuation of the Bible among Dalits. It was not as if they merely did not have the sacred text; instead it was that they were refused it because such a pure form of divine revelation could not be placed close to their polluted being. Kancha Ilaiah draws our attention to the manner in which the arrival of the Christian Bible transformed the identities of Dalits and Tribal communities by incorporating them into the sacred world of literacy and religious reflectivity (Ilaiah, 2004). The Bible is truly a cherished and prized concrete sacred gift, accepted by Dalit Christians as a sign of divine wisdom. The respect given to various scriptures in Asian cultures cannot be discounted in any theological process without betraying the modern or postmodern tendency to de-contextualize and de-historicize their social, psychological and religious value.

This being said, the growing influence of postcolonial biblical scholarship in Asia must also be acknowledged. Led by the substantial work of R. S. Sugirtharajah, this school of theology represents quite a different mood and mode of operation. It has helped sceptically and deliberately to undo colonial interpretations of Scripture and a Western exegesis that justifies domination. As a first step, 'the hermeneutics of suspicion' thus dislocated the colonizer from his or her privileged position of weaving a biblical master narrative that fuelled Asian theology. Thereafter, in a second step referred to as 'the hermeneutics of recovery and transfiguration', diverse native voices deliberately disabled the position of the colonizer as the subject of a Christian world-view that was once taken for granted as 'real' and skilfully interjected their own 'othered' identities as the authors of a more authentic

Asian-Christian world-view. This second step can be said to have three objects. First, it excavates testimonials of the agency of colonized, marginalized and dominated peoples from within the archives of hidden history. Second, it consciously gathers together the multiple voices of such overlooked peoples, including elements both of contestation and complicity in dealing with dominant narratives. Third, postcolonial Asian scholars take into consideration the experiences of the colonized in developing perspectives which remake the future for both the subjugated and the dominant.

Conclusion

Sugirtharajah in his early, liberation-steered phase (that is before he embraced, almost completely, his Diaspora location as an alternative to his advocacy for the 'margins') reminds us of an overriding commitment as (Asian) theologians:

> When we come to decide the questions that affect our communities and our people, such as housing, health care, social security, education or homeland, the relevant questions will be about how they affect the lives of the people rather than whether the proposal is modern or non-modern, colonial or anti-colonial. The task of postcolonialism is to ensure that the yearnings of the poor take precedence over the interests of the affluent, that the emancipation of the subjugated has primacy over the freedom of the powerful, and that the participation of the marginalized takes priority over the perpetuation of the system which systematically excludes them. (Sugirtharajah, 2003: 33)

I submit that Jesus gives theological legitimacy to such a radical commitment in Asian theology. The various themes discussed in this essay make it clear in many ways that Asian Christian theology is committed to transforming life for all human beings, even while it groans for the restoration of the entire cosmos. No doubt this can be achieved through collaboration with all religious communities. A universal God wills this for the common human community. Yet the specifically Christian dimension that emerges through such reflections is the significance of Jesus Christ, who through his solidarity with the poor and marginalized shapes and propels this theological vision to achieve fullness of life of all. It is because of this solidarity, manifest in God-become-flesh, that the fluidity, tentativeness and abstraction of theology, Christology and biblical studies are committed fully to the liberation of the excluded, poor and colonized.

❓ SUGGESTED QUESTIONS

1 What are the five dimensions in the method of doing Christian theology in Asia? How do they help you express your Christian faith?

2 What are the three important themes pursued by Christian theology in Asia? How relevant are they to your context?

3 Explain the idea of 'divine spaciousness'. Are you comfortable with this idea, which seeks to have an open attitude towards neighbours of different faiths? What sorts of practices might this idea of divine spaciousness imply for you in your context?

2
Interfaith dialogue and Christian theology in Asia

Edmund Kee-Fook Chia

 Abstract

In this essay Chia defines interfaith as the act of reaching across to people who express their concern for the world and for life and its meaning in ways different from us, and dialogue as conversation which is honest, sincere and civil, which is both formal and informal, verbal and non-verbal. He summarizes the historical developments, particularly the influence of Western Christianity, which have increased the importance in Asia of interfaith dialogue. Finally he highlights four salient forms of interfaith dialogue in Asia, namely dialogue of life, dialogue of action, dialogue of discourse and dialogue of spirituality, all of which have different aims and objectives and need to be adapted by Asians in ways appropriate to their own contexts.

 Interfaith dialogue: definition of terms

The term 'interfaith dialogue' is bandied around in so many circles today that it is important for us to define it from the outset. It is used generally to signify the activity of dialogue among people or institutions across faith lines. In order to appreciate what this means, let us begin by breaking down the term 'interfaith dialogue' into the two words 'interfaith' and 'dialogue'.

By interfaith we simply mean between different faith traditions. The term faith, as opposed to religion, is used intentionally so as not to exclude those who do not wish to be associated with religion in its institutional forms. In the Asian context this is especially significant since some religions, such as Confucianism and even at times Buddhism, are often viewed more as a philosophy of life. Interfaith, therefore, is the act of reaching across to persons who express their concern for the world and for life and its meaning in ways different from ours.

The word dialogue as used in the context of interfaith dialogue is more complex than it seems. Dialogue, in the words of American Catholic theologian Leonard Swidler, is 'conversation between two or more persons with differing views, the primary purpose of which is for each participant to learn from the other so that he or she can change and grow' (Swidler, 1990: 3). In short, dialogue, unlike debate, is a constructive activity, aimed at promoting positive relationships. It is 'conversation' in that those engaged in it are doing so not to attack or condemn each other but to have an honest, sincere and civil exchange. These exchanges can be verbal, but they can also be nonverbal. They can be formal, but they can also be informal.

In the interfaith context, dialogue includes interactions beyond the oral or even the written form. Dialogue can take the form of encounters where no words are exchanged but a lot else is happening. These may be activities as mundane as just being present to another, or exchanges of smiles and affirming gestures, or a helping hand in time of need.

> Therefore, dialogue essentially means encounters between peoples of different faiths that both promote better understandings of each other and nurture positive relationships with each other.

Each dialogue partner communicates not only something about his or her own faith but also that his or her faith is respectful of the faith of the other.

Interfaith dialogue: a Western agenda?

It may come as a surprise that, even though most of the world's major religious and spiritual traditions have roots in Asia, the agenda of interfaith dialogue is often perceived as a Western enterprise. To be sure, it came to prominence in theological discourse through the writings of Western scholars such as Wilfred Cantwell Smith, Hans Küng, John Hick, Paul Knitter and Leonard Swidler, among a host of other Christian theologians. Why is this so? How come Asia was not the place which gave birth to the activity of interfaith dialogue? Let me attempt an initial response to these questions by means of a personal anecdote.

Several years ago Pope John Paul II invited religious leaders from various parts of the world to Rome for an interfaith assembly to pray for peace. This came shortly after the atrocities surrounding the events of September 11 and October 7, 2001. September 11, of course, represents the beginning of what in some quarters is regarded as the 'war on America', when commercial aeroplanes were flown into civilian targets in the USA. For those on the other side of the divide, October 7 (the day the first depleted-uranium bombs were dropped on Afghanistan) represents the start of the 'war on

Islam' and is seen as the more abominable and ruthless act, as leaders of a so-called 'civilized' nation targeted countless numbers of helpless Afghan women and children who had nothing to do with the atrocities of September 11. In any case, an interfaith dialogue assembly was summoned as a result of these tense events. The absence of peace was the immediate driving force behind the assembly.

Since I was at that time working for the Church in Asia, specifically in the field of interfaith dialogue, a journalist from Europe contacted me to ask: 'Why is it that you guys in Asia, where there are so many religions, do not bother to have interfaith dialogue assemblies the way we have them in Rome?' My response to that innocent question went something like this: 'Let me explain why by recounting to you my experience as a teacher of the English language in my home country, Malaysia, where not many people use the language. As part of my duties to promote its use, I organized a monthly Speak English Day when we would have events such as the singing of English songs, the recitation of English poems, board games such as Scrabble played in English, and all sorts of other activities with English as the medium of communication. Now, why is it that in England, where so many people speak English, no one bothers to organize a Speak English Day?'

> In a way what has been called interfaith dialogue in the West is something which Asians participate in on a daily basis.

To the extent that it is routine it no longer constitutes a special activity. This is because, since most countries in Asia are religiously plural, Asians have almost no choice but to be engaged with people of religions other than their own. These encounters occur on a daily basis, in the workplace and the marketplace, rather than in artificially organized assemblies and forums held in conference halls. One could even say that interfaith dialogue has become so much a part of Asian life that it is a constituent element of the Asian psyche. To be sure, many Asian Christians have relatives or even spouses, children or parents, who adhere to another religion. An ordinary family gathering is already an interfaith dialogue assembly! Thus, there is really no need for specially constructed interfaith dialogue activity, for there is already a natural interfaith dimension in people's daily lives.

The same cannot be said of the West, which historically has been homogenously Christian. Even though people of other religions have been living there for millennia, their presence was so insignificant that they were almost invisible in public life. It is only in the last half-century or so, with the advent of the global economy and communication, trans-continental travel and exchanges, and the influx of immigrants from the East to the West, that Westerners have for the first time experienced first-hand what Asians have been living with for millennia. And since this is a new phenomenon for the hitherto Christian West, Western Christians more or less 'invented' interfaith dialogue in order to deal with the new social order attendant upon their communities.

Western Christianity in Asia

Having said all of the above, I will now make a case for the importance of interfaith dialogue in the Asian context. While it is true that the experience of religious pluralism is very much ingrained within the Asian psyche, it is also true that this has only been explicitly brought into conscious awareness very recently. Perhaps experiences deemed natural and ordinary often escape people's conscious awareness, much in the way that a fish does not know what water is. It is no surprise then that Asian Christians never talked about interfaith dialogue until Western Christians began examining the issue.

This is in part because the history of Christianity in Asia, during the last five hundred years in particular, has been actually not so much a history of Asian Christianity but one of Western Christianity as played out on Asian soil – with the exception of the indigenous Orthodox traditions. The issues of concern to Christians in Asia, therefore, were those of their mother Church in Europe. To be sure, Asian Christianity held on to so many of the characteristics of its mother churches that local churches in Asia were like little English, Dutch, French, Portuguese or Spanish churches. One could even say that churches in Asia were 'colonies' of European churches. As a result Asians in general looked upon Christianity as a foreign religion. In my own national Malay language Christianity is often described as the *agama orang putih* (literally: white man's religion). This sentiment remains even today, since in most countries the vestiges of European Christianity linger on.

Furthermore, it doesn't help that Christianity was actually spread to Asia in concert with the programme of colonial expansion (Evers, 2005). The Church is therefore inevitably associated with the imperial powers who, in the eyes of Asians, came primarily for the conquest of their lands. The Cross of Christ accompanied the swords, the guns and the looting barrels in what Sri Lankan theologian Aloysius Pieris calls the 'unholy alliance of the missionary, the military and the merchant' (Pieris, 1988: 50). Just as the imperialists' aim was the plunder of the resources of Asia, Christianity was viewed as coming to plunder the souls of the peoples of Asia. The late Indian theologian Stanley Samartha illustrates this situation appropriately by drawing an analogy with the arrival of a helicopter in Asia. When descending upon Asia – from above, of course – the helicopter blew away all that was on the ground, paving the way for the European Church to land (Samartha, 1991: 115).

It didn't matter what the other religions stood for; they were to be wiped out. There was no way Christianity would tolerate these heathen and pagan religions, let alone respect them or be nourished by them. Christianity had to be transplanted into Asia, where it was expected to take root and bear the same fruits as it did across the European continent.

> Western Christianity thought that there was only one fate for the adherents of other religions in Asia; they were to be converted.

In such an era Christian missionaries 'often adopted the attitude that non-Christian religions were simply the work of Satan and the missionaries' task was to convert from error to knowledge of the truth' (cited in Pope Paul VI, 1966: n. 11). This was in essence the theology of other religions that Asian Christians were brought up to subscribe to for most of the 500-year history of Christianity in Asia.

 ## The advent of Asian Christianity

Things began to change, however, in the middle of the twentieth century. The year 1945 is often regarded as the watershed for this transition. With the end of the Second World War and the Pacific War in Asia and with the subsequent dismantling of colonialism, the indigenous peoples of former colonies began to rise up not only against political oppression but also in search of their own indigenous identities. In the words of Samartha:

> Deep down, it is a struggle for identity, a quest for spiritual resources in the fight against injustice. The rejection of religious pluralism, the refusal to recognize that neighbours of other faiths in the world live by their own cherished beliefs and values, is a more serious form of injustice than the merely economic.
>
> (Samartha, 1991: 2)

Thus began what was to become a search not only for indigenous identities but also for the resources which help give shape to these identities. The Asian religious traditions are a significant factor among these resources. It is no coincidence that the expulsion of Christian missionaries alongside the imperial governors from many countries in Asia was followed by a revival in the Asian religions. This happened all across Asia, thus bringing Asian religions to the consciousness of the global communities. It was then that Westerners began to notice the contribution of Buddhism to the lives of the people in Sri Lanka or Thailand, of Hinduism to those in India or Nepal, and of Islam to those in Bangladesh or Indonesia. In some instances this resurgence swung the pendulum to the other extreme (as a form of catharsis against the many years of suppression during the colonial era), with the result that the more extremist forms of these religious traditions came to the fore. This effect continues today and it will be several decades more before the catharsis is complete.

This movement of revivalism or resurgence in Asian religions did not go unnoticed by the local Christians. Influenced by the mood and spirit of the times, they too began a quest for their own identity, one which could be at once truly Christian and truly Asian. Among the more significant issues in this quest was Christianity's relation with other religions. This was by no means an abstract theological issue to be discussed but one which had concrete and dire consequences for the lives of Asian Christians. This is because most Christians in Asia have roots in these other religions or family members who still adhere to them. While in the past Asian Christians were informed by a theology which speculated that all their loved ones were destined to hell unless they were baptized, the quest for a truly Asian Christianity opened up new horizons for a theology which was not only more respectful of other religions but also enabled them to be perceived in a more positive light.

An Asian theology of interfaith dialogue

The one event which provided the greatest impetus to the development of Asian Christianity within the Roman Catholic Church was the Second Vatican Council, popularly known as Vatican II. One of the more succinct ways to summarize the changes which the Council brought about is by reference to the encyclical *Ecclesiam Suam*, issued by Pope Paul VI in 1964. In *Ecclesiam Suam* (its English title is 'Paths of the Church'), Paul delineates ways in which the Church must carry out its mission in the contemporary world (Pope Paul VI, 1964). He spells this out in its many aspects but they can all be captured by one word, namely 'dialogue'. By dialogue, Paul refers to the four categories or levels of dialogue which the Church should be engaged in: dialogue with the world and cultures, dialogue with other religions, dialogue with other Christians, and dialogue within the Church (Chia, 2001: xiv).

It was this spirit of dialogue which saw Catholics in Asia shift their theological concerns to focus on the reality of the many poor, the many cultures, and the many religions to be found in the Asian context. In the realm of theology this dialogue resulted in what is today known as the Theology of Other Religions or the Theology of Interfaith Dialogue. This theology takes as its starting point Vatican II's document *Nostra Aetate*, the 'Declaration on the Relationship of the Church to Non-Christian Religions'. In particular, the following article was revolutionary, at least by the ecclesial standards of the 1960s:

> The Catholic Church rejects nothing which is true and holy in these religions. She looks with sincere respect upon those ways of conduct and of life, those rules and teachings which, though differing in many particulars from what

she holds and sets forth, nevertheless often reflect a ray of that Truth which enlightens all men. (Pope Paul VI, 1966: 2)

While it was Vatican II that officially 'canonized' the exploration of the Church's relation with other religions, it was the Asian Church, as represented by the Federation of Asian Bishops' Conferences (FABC), which played the most significant role. At the very first FABC Plenary Assembly in 1974, in discussing the theme of 'Evangelization in Modern Day Asia', the bishops defined the task of evangelization in Asia as follows:

> In Asia especially this involves a dialogue with the great religious traditions of our peoples. In this dialogue we accept them as significant and positive elements in the economy of God's design of salvation. In them we recognize and respect profound spiritual and ethical meanings and values. Over many centuries they have been the treasury of the religious experience of our ancestors, from which our contemporaries do not cease to draw light and strength. They have been (and continue to be) the authentic expression of the noblest longings of their hearts, and the home of their contemplation and prayer. They have helped to give shape to the histories and cultures of our nations.
> (FABC, 1997: art. 14)

The Bishops then revealed their own position by asking, albeit rhetorically, 'How then can we not give them reverence and honor? And how can we not acknowledge that God has drawn our peoples to Himself through them?' (FABC, 1997: art. 15). This 1974 statement, together with the many subsequent statements of the FABC, provided the necessary endorsement by the magisterium of the Church in Asia to Asian theologians as they went about their reflections on a theology of interfaith dialogue. Since then Asian Christians have been engaged in interfaith dialogue as part of their evangelizing mission and have seen it as integral to their existence as Christians in Asia. These dialogue engagements have taken on many forms and involve every Christian in Asia.

 ## Forms of interfaith dialogue in Asia

Interfaith dialogue in Asia, therefore, is not confined to formal discussions about faith or religion. It takes on multiple forms, employs multiple means, and is engaged in at multiple levels. It is meant for everyone, and every person has a right as well as a duty to be involved in it. What is essential to note is that there are different types or levels of dialogue and people are involved at the level they find themselves most suited for.

At the most basic level is what is called the *dialogue of life*. This is the dialogue which happens in day-to-day life, among ordinary people on the streets. This dialogue takes place whenever spiritual and human values shape people's day-to-day interactions with their neighbours of other faiths. It may be as simple as a mother teaching her children to show respect for people of another faith or a taxi driver going out of his way to return a lost suitcase to a passenger of another faith. It is also manifested when a teacher shows love, dedication and attention to students irrespective of their religious affiliation or when a resident is considerate and helpful to a neighbour of a different faith tradition. The dialogue of life, therefore, is the most important type of interfaith dialogue and, ideally, all other forms of dialogue should lead to or be augmented by it.

When people of different faith traditions come together to address some common social or communal concern they are engaged in what is called the *dialogue of action*. Problems posed by the AIDS epidemic, poverty, drug addiction, gangsterism, illiteracy, the exploitation of people in general, and ecological rape are some of the issues addressed by the dialogue of action. It is considered interfaith dialogue insofar as the parties involved are consciously collaborating with one another on account of their faith and despite their differences. The collaborative venture provides an avenue for the dialogue partners to witness each other's faith in action and to discern common elements which undergird their respective traditions.

A third level is what is called the *dialogue of discourse*. Also referred to as the dialogue of theological exchange or the dialogue of experts, this dialogue often takes place at a formal level among specialists or trained scholars or leaders of the various faith traditions. It can take place in oral or written form, occurring in the latter through the exchange of words in books and journals or even emails, tweets and weblogs. Because of its high profile many people mistakenly think of this form of dialogue whenever reference is made to interfaith dialogue. The dialogue of discourse, no doubt, has its value and function and provides the necessary data for other forms of dialogue to feed on.

A fourth kind of dialogue is what is referred to as the *dialogue of spirituality*. Here the dialogue is concerned with the spiritual dimensions of one's faith. How do we pray? why do we pray? who is God to us? what motivates us to live virtuously? are some of the questions addressed in this kind of dialogue. The contents of the dialogue of spirituality may include our experiences on pilgrimage, a spiritual insight, a religious vision or a prayer image. Instead of relying on words, the dialogue of spirituality can also take the form of actually sharing with one another different spiritual experiences. Coming together in prayer and meditation is the most common example of the dialogue of spirituality. While monks, nuns, mystics, Sufis and saddhus play a significant role in this dialogue, it is open to all, as long as those involved are open to crossing over in order to experience the spirituality of the dialogue partner.

As can be seen from the foregoing examples, there are different types or levels of dialogue. They have different aims and are targeted at different clusters of people. All people of faith should be involved in dialogue at one level or another and it is only when dialogue becomes a *habitus*, a way of life, that societies can claim to be truly interfaith communities. Such is the aim of the Asian approach to a Christian theology of other religions and such ought to be the aspiration of every Christian in Asia.

 SUGGESTED QUESTIONS

1 What are the different levels at which dialogue can happen in the Asian context? What is your own engagement with dialogue?

2 Do you think interfaith dialogue comes from a Western agenda?

3 What is the importance of interfaith dialogue in a multi-faith context like Asia? In what way is it significant in your own particular context?

3
Asian Christian liberation theology
Philip Vinod Peacock

 Abstract

In this essay Peacock recognizes that since resources for liberation in the Asian context can be found not only in Christianity but also in other faith traditions, there is a need for Asian Christian theology to be in dialogue with those faith traditions. Furthermore, he understands liberation theology in terms of the Latin American liberation theologian Gustavo Gutiérrez's definition of it as a theology of conflict and reflects upon the variety of conflict situations from which Asian liberation theologies emerged in various forms – as theologies of resistance to colonialism, patriarchy, poverty, dehumanization and social exclusion.

 Introduction

Writing an essay on Asian liberation theology is not an easy task. Not only for the reason that Asia is an ambiguous concept, geographically, politically and culturally, but also because any essay on Asian liberation theology has to provide an account of theological expression that spreads over two centuries – for, after all, the earliest articulations of Asian liberation theology can be found in responses to colonialism.

Speaking from the perspective of Asia, with its religious diversity, it is immediately necessary to state that this essay will limit itself to Asian Christian liberation theology. To do so is respectfully to submit that religious resources for liberation are not the exclusive preserve of Christian theology but are also found in other Asian faith traditions. The Sri Lankan theologian Aloysius Pieris would in fact argue that Asian theology has to move between the two poles of the 'Third Worldness of our continent and its particularly Asian character' (Pieris, 1988: 67). He goes on to define the. 'Third Worldness' of Asia as poverty and 'its particularly Asian character' as its religiosity; or, as Paul Knitter puts it in the foreword to the same book, 'the question of the many poor and the question of the many religions' (Pieris, 1988: 1). This implies that

> Asian Christian liberation theology must not only be cognizant of the emergence of liberation theology from other faith traditions but also of the necessity for an authentic Asian Christian liberation theology to be in dialogue with these other faith traditions.

This essay therefore will attempt to offer the reader a general overview of what can be termed Asian Christian liberation theology.

Liberation as a Christian theological project evolved out of a dissatisfaction with the social, economic, political and ideological concept of development. Interestingly, according to Gustavo Gutiérrez, it was the Bandung Conference of 1955, in which the leaderships of Asian and African countries met, that contributed to the understanding of Third World countries as 'underdeveloped' (Gutiérrez, 1974: 23). To Gutiérrez and other liberation theologians, however, the term development is timid and 'aseptic, giving a false picture of a tragic and conflictual reality', and is contrary to liberation, which emphasizes the reality of conflict between nations, classes and humans in the context of the historical socio-economic and political relations that exist between them. Liberation theology is further defined as theological reflection on this conflict (Gutiérrez, 1974: 26, 35, 36).

Having defined liberation theology as theological reflection on conflict, I will now attempt to offer an overview of how Asian Christian theologians have attempted to reflect theologically on conflict. I will specifically look at various categories of resistance: resistance to colonialism, resistance to patriarchy, resistance to poverty, resistance to dehumanization and resistance to social exclusion.

It should be stated at the outset that we should use these categories with caution and try to avoid oversimplifying them. While such categories are useful for the purpose of study and therefore have their place in a study guide such as this, one should be aware of the complexity of Asian Christian liberation theology.

 ## Resistance to colonialism

Perhaps the first expressions of an Asian Christian liberation theology were part of the resistance to colonialism. If there is an experience in Asia common to all its inhabitants it would probably be that of colonialism. Colonialism has had a deep and devastating impact on Asia, and its effects can be seen even today. While Asia and Europe probably began the transition into modernity at the same time, they did so in entirely different ways, one

Asian Christian liberation theology

as the colonizer and the other as the colonized. Colonialism impacted Asia economically, politically, socially and psychologically.

Economically, colonialism meant nothing but the extraction of raw materials from Asia in order for the West to create wealth. This process was devastating to local economies, which as a result of colonialism were overturned to become producers of raw materials for consumers in Europe.

Politically, colonialism meant for the colonized the loss of the right to self-rule and self-determination. In the late nineteenth and twentieth century opposition to colonial imperialism took the form of nationalism, which attempted to confront empire using the Western entity of the nation state. The process was not without its own difficulties and new studies of nationalism are discovering that it often served to crystallize the dominance of the local elite, who, even if they opposed colonial imperialism, colluded for their own purposes with colonial interests and colonial ideology. The end of imperialism for many powerless groups across Asia merely meant, therefore, the handing over of the reins of power to new masters.

Socially, the colonial powers often colluded with local dominant communities in ways that served either to ratify ancient hierarchies, reinvent them in new ways or create entirely new ones. Essentially colonialism meant that vulnerable groups, particularly women, peasants, small artisans, indigenous people and those at the bottom of social hierarchies, became even more vulnerable.

Psychologically, colonialism was constructed and imagined as a sense of loss and defeat, as entailing even the emasculation of the colonized. Colonialism was after all not merely the extraction of wealth but also a clash of ideas within which certain ideologies, for example scientific rationalism, were privileged over others. This sense of loss and emasculation continues to exhibit itself in various ways including the glorification of violence, colonial constructions of knowledge and the imagining of a glorious past that itself has problematic implications today. There is of course significant work being done by Asians today in the field of postcolonialism that seeks to critically examine some of these issues.

It is significant that early responses to colonialism took the form of cultural critique. Colonial imperialism came with an imperial theology that discounted, discredited and delegitimized native religious traditions while at the same time privileging itself as the natural state of affairs. It was in this context that early Asian Christian thinkers, for example Indian theologians such as Krishna Mohun Banerjea and Brahmabandhab Upadhyay, began to use native theological categories in their own processes of theological thinking. While there is a tendency to read such early attempts at theologizing, using Hindu resources to explain Christian theological formulations, as indigenization or inculturation that overlooked socio-political reality, such a reading is naïve and simplistic. Read within the context of colonialism, such theologies played a counter-cultural role, seeking to give value to the culture of the native while at the same time delegitimizing the culture of the colonizer. Seen within the context of the clash of ideas, this form of theologizing – which later came to be categorized as Indian Christian theology – was a theological reflection on the cultural dominance of the colonizer in conflict with local cultures and identities.

Cultural expressions of theology were however not restricted to India, nor are they only to be found within the context of Western colonialism. On the one hand there seems to be a resurgence of cultural theologizing in east Asia, particularly in Taiwan and to some extent in Indonesia; the Taiwanese theologian Huang Po Ho, for example, writes extensively about the need to use local cultural expressions in Asian Christian liberation theologies.

On the other hand the theology of Asia's indigenous people falls back on their cultural heritage to evoke metaphors and symbols deeply critical of the neo-colonial ideologies that seek to extinguish them. From north-east India, the Mizo theologians use the concept of *tlawmngaihna* and the Ao Nagas use that of *sobaliba*, both of which reflect different aspects of community living in order to counter not only the impact of modernization but also the cultural hegemony of the Indian state.

There are however several difficulties with this approach. First is the entire question of the dualism that exists between culture and reason; while there is no doubt that this is a product of the colonial imagination, the fact remains that it is Asian theologies that are seen to be cultural while the theologies that emerge from the West are seen to be rational. Second, Asian theologians have been captive to a colonial habit of essentialism and homogenization in their understanding of culture. The danger of such essentialism and homogenization was the tendency of those who theologized to use the cultural elements of the local elite and oppressor. Therefore while some of these cultural theologies played the role of a counter-theology to colonialism, they continued to legitimize the role of the local power-holders. Moreover, in some instances what has been understood as native culture has in itself been a colonial construct, for example the understanding of Hinduism used by the early Indian Christian theologians.

There have, however, also been Asian theologians who have avoided this pitfall. Theologians like Kwok Pui-lan and Chung Hyun Kyung, for example, have resisted the temptation of essentialism and have instead used the actual experience of women in Asia, from which an alternative theology of resistance is evoked. Kwok Pui-lan and R. S. Sugirtharajah have also used postcolonial methods to respond to and analyse the cultural legacy of colonialism and to re-inspire theology from this perspective.

Resistance to patriarchy

Emerging as a significant theological expression in Asia is Asian feminist theology, or – as its practitioners often prefer to call it – Asian women's theology. This theology emerges from resistance to patriarchy as a system that controls the labour, fertility and sexuality of women. Described by both Kwok Pui-lan and Chung Hyun Kyung as a cry, or a plea, to God that arises out of the pain of Asian women, Asian women's theology finds its roots in the anti-imperial struggle in which women worked along with men to overthrow colonialism.

> Asian women's theology has developed in its critical expression as a theology of life that not only takes into consideration injustice based on gender discrimination but also engages with issues of poverty, ecological crises, social exclusion and political domination in a way that makes clear the connections between these various forms of oppression.

Asian women's theology has reclaimed the central place of women's experience in theological expression and biblical interpretation. Rereading the Bible from the perspective of Asian women has creatively offered alternative interpretations that seek to highlight the significant contributions of women within the text as well as in the context, while at the same time throwing light on issues that have not been raised by patriarchal interpreters of the Bible.

 ## Resistance to poverty

Another common experience across Asia is that of poverty. It would be naïve for us to suggest that poverty in Asia is the result of colonialism; to take the view that this state of affairs can be attributed to a single cause is too simplistic. However what we must also realize is that the logic of the present economic order, in placing value on profit over people, has only served to exacerbate poverty. The situation is made worse by state and non-state actors, such as international financial bodies and transnational corporations, who press for a particular economic model that would benefit the powerful while wreaking havoc with the lives of the powerless. This neo-liberal agenda is being pushed via structural adjustment programmes that seek to privatize, liberalize and globalize the economy, subsuming all activities to the logic of profit making. Unemployment, the reduction of workers' rights and an increasing gap between the rich and the poor are the results of this.

Theological reflections on poverty have in many ways been the hallmark of Asian liberation theologies. Picking up their cue from liberation theology that was evolving in South America, Asian theologians also identified the importance of poverty. Several common themes emerge in Asian Christian theological reflections on poverty. First is the importance of social analysis. Almost all articles and books on Asian Christian liberation theology begin with an analysis of contemporary society in both historical and structural perspective. John Mohan Razu, for example, in his book *Global Capitalism as Hydra*, a work rooted in Marxist social analysis, adopts an ethical point of view to describe and analyse globalization from below, demonstrating the death-dealing blows that the modern market system lands on the poor. In Asian Christian liberation theology social analysis is integral to the process of theologizing and is its necessary prerequisite. While most Asian Christian liberation theology, and particularly that emerging in the 1970s and the early 1980s, has used Marxism as a tool of analysis (many practitioners being influenced by the framework for analysing society developed by Françoise Houtart, which has its roots in Marxism), not all has been captive to this method. Aruna Gnanadasson, for example, has used as a means of social analysis the lens of eco-feminism, through which she critiques the patriarchal, capitalist war machine that oppresses both women and the earth.

A second theme often found in Asian theological reflections on poverty is critical reflection on colonial pietistic theologies. Noting that theology in Asia emerged as part of a colonial enterprise that sought to depoliticize the native populations and was used as a tool of subjugation, Asian liberation theology criticizes attempts to call people to disengage with the world and not question the violence of the system that creates poverty.

> Instead Asian Christian liberation theology calls people to actively engage with the world through solidarity with the poor, not as a means of romanticizing poverty but as a means of protest.

A related recurring theme is the constant call to engage with grassroots people's movements, their struggles being the substance from which theology is developed. In this sense liberation theology in Asia does not only see itself as being concerned with words about God but as critical engagement with the world as a means to its transformation. Aloysius Pieris, for example, speaks about the spiritual value of voluntary poverty as a way of resisting poverty itself.

A third theme that can be found in Asian theological reflections on poverty is the redemptive potential of the poor. Instead of seeing them as objects, of charity or otherwise, Asian Christian theology sees the poor as subjects of history and as being the very means of salvation of the world. The poor in Asian Christian liberation theology are identified as the agents of salvation in the world, and in this sense the poor take on a messianic role for the salvation of the whole of humanity. It is often stressed that one's salvation depends on one's relationship with the poor.

A fourth theme found in Asian Christian liberation theology is the suffering of God. In the context of Asian poverty God is not imagined as being immune to injury but instead as suffering and feeling pain. Allan J. Delotavo, for example, writing about the images of Christ in Filipino culture, cites the suffering Christ as the religiously most prominent image among the Filipinos.

Likewise other Asian Christian theologians have reflected on the theme of Christ as a co-sufferer, one who feels the people's pain. While younger theologians are now questioning the efficacy of a co-sufferer in bringing salvation from suffering, none the less their discussions too are in essence reflections on suffering.

Connected with resistance to poverty, and probably emerging at the same time, is what we may categorize as resistance to dehumanization, defined as the devaluing of human life.

 Resistance to dehumanization

Resistance to dehumanization has taken very distinct forms within the context of Asian Christian liberation theology. In its first form it is of course a theological reflection that emerges out of resistance to political domination. Within the Asian context, two particular theologies arise out of the devaluing of human life as a result of political domination. The first, emerging out of the context of the struggle for democracy in South Korea, is Minjung theology. Literally translated, the Korean word *Minjung* comes from *Min*, 'people' and *jung*, 'mass', and therefore means 'mass of the people'. Often identified with the poor, the Minjung were also those who were politically oppressed. Minjung theology is a people's theology that 'is an accumulation and articulation of theological reflection on the political experiences in the Korean situation today' (Suh, 1983: 17–18).

Another theology of resistance to dehumanization that we must also consider is Palestinian liberation theology, which arises out of the experiences of the Palestinian people who have been colonized by Israel. Central to this theological formulation is the critical examination of Christian theology that has been used to legitimize Israel's occupation of Palestine.

In speaking of a theology of resistance to dehumanization, the name M. M. Thomas immediately comes to mind. For Thomas sin and salvation are to be read in terms of the loss and regaining of humanity. For Thomas, although salvation is not identical with humanization it is integrally linked with it. The difficulty with Thomas's understanding of humanization, however, is that he makes it an abstract concept rather than relating it to particular concerns and giving it specific focus. This is probably why he does not raise issues of patriarchy or social exclusion as part of his theological articulations.

 Resistance to social exclusion

In recent times a theme that has strongly appeared on the Asian theological scene is theological resistance to social exclusion – be this Dalit theology, emerging from the experiences of those who are considered to be untouchable in the Indian social hierarchy, or the theologies that emerge from reassessment of the status of disabled people in Asia. Also in a nascent stage are theologies arising from the experiences of sexual minorities and third gendered people, who also experience social exclusion.

Conclusion

Asian Christian liberation theologies have been present in the continent for over two hundred years. Mostly using experience as their regulating factor, these theologies attempt to express the theological aspirations and articulations of the many oppressed in Asia. Rooting themselves in the context and using the tools of social analysis, these theologies have been expressed in terms of the commitment of Asian theologians both to their contextual realities and to a God of justice.

SUGGESTED QUESTIONS

1 How do you understand liberation theology in the Asian context?

2 What are the various forms that liberation theology has taken in Asia? Can you draw similarities between the concerns found in the Asian context and the concerns that are prevalent in your own context?

3 What are the roles of experience and social analysis in liberation theologies in Asia? Do theologies in your own context employ tools of social analysis in their theological reflections?

4 Reflect upon the role and place of experience in contextual theologies in your own context.

4
Cross-textual hermeneutics in Asia

Archie Chi Chung Lee

Abstract

In this article Lee discusses the problems involved in the reception and interpretation of the Christian Bible in the specific multi-scriptural context of Asia. After a critical survey of two popular Asian approaches towards the Bible, namely the 'text-alone' approach and the 'text-context' interpretative mode, Lee proposes cross-textual hermeneutics as an appropriate reading strategy for the Asian context. According to Lee this cross-textual approach to reading the Bible can be applied both to reading two scriptural texts from different religious traditions together for mutual enlightenment and to reading the Bible through Asian religio-cultural texts. Furthermore, Lee argues that the cross-textual approach can enable Asian Christians to reclaim the Bible as an Asian book and thus reduce the divide between the Bible and the Asian context.

The context of cross-textual hermeneutics in Asia

Cross-textual hermeneutics is a reading strategy for the interpretation of the Christian Bible that has arisen in response to the issue of Christian identity in the particular multi-scriptural context of Asia. There is a history to the question of Asian Christian identity. It goes back to the predominantly negative attitude of Christian missionaries towards Asian culture and religion. This pejorative attitude was especially widespread and well documented during the period of Western colonial expansion in the nineteenth and early twentieth centuries. During this period, missionary ideology was largely characterized by the belief that all gentile cultures and religions were intrinsically pagan and idolatrous, if not completely savage and uncivilized.

This gospel-against-culture attitude, coupled with the traditional Western Christian denunciation of the truth-claims and values of other religious traditions, motivated many zealous and convinced young Christian men and women from the Western world to undertake the hazardous and dangerous journey overseas into the mission fields of the strange land of Asia. In most cases, the might of cannonballs made way for the arrival of the power of the Christian canon. For Asians, military humiliation was followed by iconoclastic devastation. Temples and shrines were utterly smashed. Local religious institutions and pedagogical facilities that had been housed in traditional religious sites were destroyed. Books and sacred texts were condemned, their once supreme scriptural status replaced by the Christian Bible.

For most Asian Christians, the Christian Bible is a latecomer to the continent's ancient cultural traditions. Before the Bible arrived on the shores of Asia, Asians had been nurtured for centuries by their own texts and scriptures, whose history went back to their peoples' remote past. These textual traditions are, more importantly, living and developing traditions that retain tremendous vitality to this day. They continue to shape the lives even of Asians who have been converted to Christianity. No one would imagine, for example, that Confucian, Buddhist or Taoist values and ethos would suddenly and completely disappear from Chinese people's understanding of their identity when they became Christians. Their impact has left a mark not only on the Chinese value system and the way reality is perceived, but also on the cultural identity and definition of what being a Chinese means. Although such 'scriptural' culture, in the literary sense, may not be universal in all Asian countries, it does apply to a great extent to east and south Asia. Elsewhere, religious teachings are found in oral traditions in the form of myths and songs handed down from generation to generation among aboriginal and tribal communities. Yet, either in written or oral form, Asian culture is characterized by a multiplicity and diversity of religious traditions and spiritualities grounded in age-long history and culture.

> In encountering the new textual tradition of the Bible, Asian Christians inevitably read it by way of the native cultural text they have in their possession and interpret it from the perspective of the Asian cultural tradition in which they have been brought up.

The rich variety of Asian scriptures and cultural classics constitute the lens through which the Bible is to be read meaningfully and relevantly. The religious-symbolic system, the core values of society and the ethical codes of their own cultural configuration are the resources through which Asian Christians will have come to terms with the Bible. These are embedded in Asian languages and the Asian cultural ethos. In the process of translating the Bible into Asian languages, a variety of crossovers and transformations have inevitably come into play. Cross-textual hermeneutical strategy, which has been adopted by Asian biblical scholars in the past two decades, has proved to be an appropriate method for dealing with the multi-scriptural context of Asia (Lee, 2008).

Other textual approaches to dealing with the Asian reality

A cross-textual hermeneutical strategy aims at dealing with the failure of some past and current approaches to the Bible to pay attention to the cultural text. These approaches include (1) *the text-alone approach*, which is designed to lift up understanding of the Bible as the absolute, authoritative revelation of God in history; and (2) *the text-context interpretative mode*, which is intended to locate the biblical text in an Asian context in order that the Christian message can be heard and understood.

The 'text-alone' approach sees and reads the Bible as the only 'text' to be venerated as the timeless, universal, self-sufficient and unchanging record of God. Here, biblical interpretation does not play any significant role at all. In the tradition of the Church, it is usually the doctrinal affirmation attached to the text, rather than the Bible itself, that dominates and shapes the interpretation. The historical-critical approach, which has long been practised in academia, also falls within this category. Scholars using this method mostly assume that one can thereby obtain an objective and scientific result in understanding the historical background and constructing the meaning of the biblical text accordingly. The role of the reader and his or her social location is assumed to have to be eliminated from the interpretation process. What is in and behind the text is the only thing that really matters. Readers who are in favour of this approach claim that their interpretation of the biblical text is of absolute validity and primary authority for all peoples. The Asian socio-political context and cultural-religious experience are not brought into the picture and have no bearing on the task of reading the Bible. Some peculiar usages of language and cultural characteristics are incorporated only as illustrations and for the purpose of effectively communicating the core message of the gospel.

The 'text-context' approach is one attempt to react to the failure of the 'text-only' method to recognize the importance of context in reading the Bible. It takes the interpreter's context seriously and sees the text as requiring interpretation in that context. Asian scholars have arrived at an awareness of the importance of Asian contexts in interpreting the biblical text. There is a strong commitment to contextual hermeneutics among Asian biblical scholars and theologians who take the biblical text seriously in their theological reflections. It is admitted that every text has its own original context, and that it also possesses the ability to adapt to new contexts. Attention is paid to the levels of meaning located at different stages of the formation of the canon. The aim of biblical interpretation then becomes both to grasp the meaning of a text within its life history for former generations, and also to search for its contemporary theological significance for readers in their social locations. This twofold task of explaining 'what a text meant' in biblical time and 'what it means today' is, therefore, often understood as the main responsibility of biblical interpretation.

Some Asian scholars, however, are uncomfortable with the 'text-context' interpretative mode, as it assumes that the context is only the medium of transmission of the Bible. Context is void of any significant content that contributes to the interpretation process. D. Perman Niles calls for the reconsideration of the fact that context is not simply a thing, 'a mere conglomeration of Asian realities', but 'the people themselves who live amongst these realities' (Niles, 1985: 282). Indeed, since the context has multiple texts that contribute to the reading of the Bible, we have to acknowledge that context is a text that may speak to the Bible. It inevitably has something to contribute to the reshaping of the biblical text.

Asian scholars also find the text-context interpretative mode inadequate in the multi-religious context of Asia. It has ignored the existence of Asian sacred scriptures and the Asian life experience.

> Asian Christians have in fact two identities: an Asian cultural identity and a Christian identity. We Asians are also aware that we live in two worlds: the world of the Bible and Christian faith and the world of Asian scriptures, cultures and religions. Both identities and both worlds should be upheld in a creative, dynamic, interrelated, interactive and integrated way, so that integrity is safeguarded.

We Asian Christians, therefore, have constantly to struggle with this double/dual identity and come to terms with the two 'texts' entrusted to us: the Asian 'text' that we have inherited from our own Asian cultural-religious traditions and the biblical 'text' we have received from the Judaeo-Christian communities. I have proposed cross-textual hermeneutics as the proper approach to solving the dilemma of Asian biblical interpretation. It gives due attention to the two texts at our disposal for doing theology and biblical studies. It is imperative that the biblical text is interpreted in our own multi-textual context in constant interpenetration and interaction with our Asian text. This third approach, cross-textual hermeneutics, tries to achieve understanding of the biblical text in relation to the cultural-religious texts of Asians and seeks to achieve interpenetration and integration of 'the two texts'.

Con/textuality and cross-textual hermeneutics

In view of the multi-textual reality of Asia, a new term should therefore be coined in recognition of the existence of Asian texts and their impact on the interpretation of the Bible. The word 'con/text' may help to illustrate the dynamics of this specific hermeneutical strategy. It points to the fact that the Asian context has a rich diversity of texts. The prefix 'con' in 'con/text' has three basic meanings: (1) as a prefix from the Latin preposition *cum*, *con*- may be attached before any consonant except b, h, l, m, p, r and w to signify 'with', 'together', 'in conjunction', 'jointly', etc.; (2) as a verb, it means to know, acknowledge, study and examine closely; and (3) as an adverb, it connotes the sense of 'against' and the 'antithesis of *pro*' (*Webster's New International Dictionary*). In coining the word 'con/text', I therefore mean to introduce the idea of both the conventional meanings of 'context' and the new meaning of the conjunction and confluence of other texts in the reading of the Bible in context. We have recognized the fact that context is never without text and is itself also a text. We are called to examine such texts closely. We also know that there are texts in that context which are not totally similar to the Bible. The existence of texts in *contrast* with the Bible has to be duly acknowledged and dealt with properly. Cross-textual reading of the Bible in Asia has to come to terms with the monotheistic/henotheistic orientation of the Bible and the polytheistic structure of Asian religious presupposition. The other important theme that potentially has an impact on biblical interpretation in Asia is the general Asian belief in the continuum between divine and human as opposed to the basic Christian theological assumption that a great divide and gulf exists between God and human.

Asian texts should be regarded as being 'on a par with' the Bible in order to bring out of the biblical text a fuller range of meanings which have been hidden or marginalized in the history of biblical interpretation. Besides placing the two texts side-by-side, cross-textual interpretation in con/text signifies the dynamic interaction with and illumination of the Bible by other Asian texts. Through such encounters, new meanings of the biblical text can be engendered, which might never have been highlighted through the reading of the Bible alone. Cross-textual interpretation also implies making crossings between the two texts during the reading process, engaging them in creative tension. In the process, the two texts should be subjected to vigorous and critical appraisal by their readers, who will seek to engage both texts so as to bring about a renewed configuration of meaning and hence a confirmation of those readers' dual identity.

A cross-textual hermeneutical approach can be applied to two major thrusts of investigation, each of which will develop into two different disciplines: (1) reading any two scriptures together in parallel for mutual enlightenment in cross-scriptural studies and (2) reading the Bible through Asian religio-cultural texts in cross-textual biblical hermeneutics. The former lays greater emphasis on the crossings and the mutual enlightenment of both texts; the latter puts its stress on the Bible and is concerned with its con/textual understanding for Asian theological construction and/or biblical interpretation. Cross-textual scriptural interpretation has suggested that there may be multiple 'crossings' between the Asian text (Text A) and the biblical text (Text B). Both texts must be read in the context of the reader, and the social location of the community must be taken into serious consideration. No one text should hold absolute sway over another, which may thereby be suppressed or silenced. There are sure to be liberating and/or enslaving elements in both texts, and the negative and enslaving elements have to be challenged and judged. Text A must be scrutinized by Text B; and, vice versa, Text B also needs to be read critically in the perspective brought to it by Text A. Each text provides the necessary contour against which the other can be seen in a proper light. It is the existence of 'the other' that strengthens the understanding of our own identity.

Finally, when it comes to adopting the cross-textual hermeneutical method of biblical interpretation, we will have to see how the Asian text would contribute to the construction of meaning for the biblical text in the con/textual setting of Asia. Asian resources, in the form of mythology (creation myths and flood stories), folktales, histories of the people, as well as stories of individual men, women and children, are of significant value to the reading process.

The two texts need to be treated as having the genuine ability to fertilize and dialogue with each other. Reading one text from the perspective of the other will then provide us with a reference point and an anchorage from which evaluation and appreciation can be made. The contour supplied by one text will furnish the backlight against which the meaning of the other text becomes more evident. The different dimensions incorporated in the complicated structure of one text can be disentangled through the numerous crossings that are presumably being made in the hermeneutical process.

The cross-textual approach also takes into consideration the interaction between the text and the reader. On the one hand, the reading process is shaped and governed by readers' social location and the power dynamics within which they are situated. Readers are in fact neither passive nor autonomous. When taking an active role in reading the biblical text, they not only bring a perspective to the interpretation of that text, they also critique the text from the perspective of their own cultural or social text. On the other hand their life will have to be examined, critiqued and claimed by the text too. Interpretations, however, must also be tested by interpreters in dialogue. The community of interpreters or 'community of inquiry', the academic and the ecclesial, must first decide on the question of how the interpretation relates intellectually and existentially to the Bible and the traditions incorporated in or tied up with it.

In reading the Bible through Asian eyes, we are encouraged to grasp the meaning of the text in the light of the people's sufferings and struggles for social justice. Perhaps these crossings, if they are genuinely executed, will help us go beyond the cultural boundary of the texts and to focus on the human quest that is common to both texts. Cross-textual hermeneutics may be a painful endeavour; it is none the less a necessity for the enrichment of both the gospel and culture.

Conclusion: Reclaiming the Christian Bible as an Asian scripture

The Christian Bible recorded the religious and socio-political experience of the people of Israel in the context of ancient Mesopotamia and Palestine. In a real sense, it originated in west Asia and travelled both eastwards and westwards. The Bible that we receive in Asia has made a detour across the Mediterranean Sea to continental Europe and Britain. When it came to Asia again during the colonial period, it had acquired and become entangled with various traditions of doctrinal interpretation from Europe and America. An Asian contribution to the hermeneutical process is therefore desirable and much to be anticipated if the Asian Christian identity is to be adequately addressed. Cross-textual interpretation in the Asian con/text is the proper way forward.

Unlike the other two ways of reading the Bible, the 'text-alone' approach and the 'text-context' mode, cross-textual reading takes seriously the distinctive religious and cultural values present in Asian classics, scriptures and social texts, and strives to integrate the divine activities in Asian history and social processes with those witnessed in the Bible. It values the common human religious quest as a necessary guiding principle for further exploration, and takes the search for the encounter with the sacred in the mundane as one of its significant presuppositions. Both the Christian text and the cultural text should be affirmed as equally significant and valid for the religious quest that they have posited and the similar human religious dimensions of life they addressed, notwithstanding differences that exist because of their varied historically and culturally bound conditions.

In the cross-textual approach, both texts must be read in the context of the reader, taking into serious consideration the social location of the community and the religious quest of the people. In this respect, the Asian text provides the necessary contour against which the former can be seen in a proper light. The two texts, both in the possession of the reader and expressing the religious experience of Asian Christians, become dialogical partners. Only in this process can Asian Christians claim the Bible as an Asian book which will then no longer be regarded as a stranger in the Asian scriptural family.

SUGGESTED QUESTIONS

1 What is cross-textual hermeneutics? Why is it relevant for the Asian context?

2 What are the two dominant approaches to the Bible followed by interpreters in the Asian context? What are their failures?

3 How can the Bible be reclaimed as an Asian scripture?

4 What are the various approaches to the Bible in your own cultural context? How do they relate to the cross-textual hermeneutical approach?

Part 2
Fighting foreign fertilizers in the furrows

5
Postcolonial Asian feminist theologies

Kwok Pui-lan

 Abstract

In her article Kwok Pui-lan explores the varied struggles of Asian women under the twofold oppression of colonialism and patriarchy. She examines how postcolonial theory has helped Asian feminist theologians to analyse the complex interaction between Asian culture and colonialism and furnishes various examples of how Asian feminist theologians have discerned and experienced the divine in the context of the struggles of Asian women by being attentive to popular literature, oral history, women's bodily experiences and issues of sexuality. She helps us to recognize how the horizons of Asian postcolonial feminist theology are being widened by the perspectives of Diaspora Asian feminists who are living outside previously colonized contexts and by understanding colonialism today in terms of the neo-liberal market economy. She concludes by pointing out the promise and potential that postcolonial theory holds for Asian feminist theologians in their twin task of gauging the present and envisioning the future.

 Introduction: postcolonial studies

Many Asian countries have undergone long periods of colonization under Japan and various European powers. Theologians in Asia thus need to scrutinize colonial experience in the past, as well as the changing economic and political situations in Asia that are a result of globalization.

> Postcolonial Asian feminist theologies aim to highlight the struggles of Asian women in different colonial contexts, analyse the collusion between patriarchy and colonialism, and lift up the theological voices of women and other marginalized peoples.

41

The term 'postcolonial' has two distinct meanings. It can be used in a temporal sense to denote the period after colonialism, when the colonized nations regained political independence. But it can also refer to a reading strategy and discursive practice that seeks to unmask Eurocentric frameworks and stereotypical cultural representations.

One of the founding texts of postcolonial studies is Edward W. Said's *Orientalism* (1978). Born of Palestinian parents, Said challenged the cultural representations of the Middle East in European scholarship and literature. His seminal text demonstrated the intimate relation between power and knowledge. Other prominent postcolonial theorists include several Asian, and particularly Indian, scholars. Gayatri Chakravorty Spivak has combined the insights of feminism, Marxism and deconstruction in her postcolonial criticism and cultural critique. Another key theorist is Homi K. Bhabha, a Parsi born in Mumbai, whose book *The Location of Culture* (1994) received critical acclaim.

 ## Asian feminist theology and postcolonial studies: the origins

When Asian feminist theology began as a grassroots movement in the late 1970s, colonialism and militarism were major concerns. During that time, the Vietnam War was raging and its effect was felt in many South-East Asian countries. Sr Mary John Mananzan OSB, a Missionary Benedictine sister from the Philippines, was a prominent critic of American imperialism and the sexual exploitation of South-East Asian women that took place around American military bases. Korean women theologians brought into the international limelight the issue of comfort women – Korean, Chinese and South-East Asian women who were forced into sexual slavery by the Japanese military during the Second World War. It was estimated that as many as 200,000 comfort women suffered from continual rape, confinement and physical abuse.

Although the early Asian feminist theological writings had clearly shown anticolonial concerns, postcolonial theory was not introduced to Asian feminist biblical studies and theology until the 1990s. The closing of an important chapter of colonial history signified by the return of Hong Kong to the Chinese in 1997 provided an occasion to reflect on the island's colonial legacy. Theologians pointed out that theology had primarily been done in the colonial centres and was therefore laden with imperializing concepts and structures. In *Discovering the Bible in the Non-Biblical World* (1995), I included a chapter on postcolonial criticism from a Hong Kong perspective. In 1998, R. S. Sugirtharajah of Sri Lanka published the first book-length study, *Asian Biblical Hermeneutics and Postcolonialism: Contesting the Interpretations*. Since then, other Asian theologians have worked on the intersection of postcolonialism and theology and biblical criticism.

Developments in postcolonial feminist theologies

Postcolonial theory provides Asian feminist theologians with critical insights on the cultural encounter between the colonizers and the colonized. Homi K. Bhabha has introduced the concepts of cultural hybridity, mimicry and ambivalence. Postcolonial Asian feminist theologians treat gospel and culture in significantly different ways than did the previous generation of Asian theologians. That generation, who came of age during Asia's struggles for independence, stressed cultural autonomy and the use of Asian religious and cultural resources in doing theology. Indigenization of the gospel in the cultural soil of Asia became a crucial theological and missiological concern. But postcolonial Asian feminist theologians challenge the generalization and simplification of Asian cultures. They also question the tendency to construct Asia and the West as binary opposites, which has the danger of replicating colonial discourse. Wai Ching Angela Wong of Hong Kong argues that it would be futile to generalize 'Asian-ness' or to reconstruct a pristine cultural past, unaffected by colonialism. For Wong, Asian cultures are cultural hybrids formed as a result of colonial contacts and there is ingenuity in the mingling. Cultures are fluid and changing and it is difficult to draw a clear boundary between what is Asian and what is Western. Thus, she questions the validity of a theological approach that promotes the use of what have been perceived as 'Asian' symbols, idioms and stories. Instead, she turns to popular literature and oral history to uncover Asian women's contemporary experience of the divine.

Colonization and militarism often reinforce male domination and misogynistic attitudes toward women. In her book *Struggle to Be the Sun Again* (1990), Chung Hyun Kyung of Korea suggests 'an epistemology of the broken body' for Asian feminist theology. Extending Chung's work, Sharon A. Bong, a Malaysian Catholic feminist theologian, uses Asian women's bodies to reimagine the suffering Christ. Bong argues that women's bodies are interpreted as markers of ethnic, cultural and religious boundaries. Thus women are more vulnerable to racism, xenophobia and related intolerance than men. But even as women suffer under multiple oppressions, they also resist, and agitate for structural changes in Church and society. Looking at Christ through the prism of Asian women's struggles and experience, Bong argues that Jesus, in suffering on the cross, at the same time reveals God's solidarity with the oppressed. Asian women imagine Christ and redemption through their embodied experience. For example, the postcolonial portrayal of Jesus as liberator, revolutionary and political martyr by Filipino women reflects their own relentless involvement in social transformation.

As part of the 'civilizing mission', the colonizers introduced to Asia their own cultural and sexual norms. Although some Asian societies might have encompassed a broader spectrum of sexual expressions, the British imposed their Victorian concepts that held heterosexuality to be the norm and promoted female domesticity. After colonialism, when the Asian male elites reasserted the value of Asian culture, there was no conscious effort to critique patriarchal biases in Asian traditions. The control of women and their sexuality became a sign that formerly colonized men had regained their manhood.

Thus, those Asian women who champion women's rights and emancipation have often been criticized as too individualistic and Westernized. Caught between tradition and modernity, many Asian women find it difficult to define their identity, especially as embodied sexual beings. The subject of women's sexuality has been a long-held taboo in many Asian Christian communities.

This taboo was challenged forcefully by Ecclesia of Women in Asia, a grassroots network of Asian Catholic women. Meeting in Yogyakarta, Indonesia, in November 2004, the group chose to discuss the theme 'Body and Sexuality' and published the proceedings afterwards. Their anthology is interdisciplinary in nature, as the authors engage biblical and theological scholarship, as well as gender theory, women's psychology, queer theory, and Asian philosophies and religions. Sexuality is not seen narrowly through a gender/sex framework, but is consistently placed within the larger cultural, political and economic contexts. Contributors are keenly aware that sexuality is shaped by a changing cultural ethos, as well as by the forces of globalization. The exploitation of women's bodies and sexuality is seen as intimately linked to women's migrancy, patriarchal business culture, and hierarchical leadership in Church and society. Yet the anthology does not treat Asian women only as victims, but also as subjects capable of seeking pleasures and expressing desires. While women's sexuality has been discussed in the Church primarily within the bounds of monogamous marriage and procreation, contributors to the anthology boldly explore other manifestations of women's passion and desire, such as lesbianism and the sexuality of older women.

In Asia, postcolonial feminist theology is not done only by women who have experienced colonialism, but also by the former colonizers. Progressive Japanese women's organizations organized a Women's International War Crimes Tribunal in 2000 and put pressure on the government to address the issue of comfort women. Hisako Kinukawa, a Japanese New Testament scholar, uses postcolonial insights to scrutinize the complexities of her place in society. As a woman in a highly patriarchal culture, she is discriminated against because of her gender. Yet, as a Japanese national, she is called to confront Japan's long history of infringing the human rights of Asian and other peoples. In her reading of biblical texts, she uses her multilayered place in society as a critical lens through which to uncover the complex power dynamics integral to them, such as class, ethnicity, urban city and rural hinterland, and Roman imperial control, in addition to gender. She stresses the importance of multi-logue (conversation with many partners) with women and men of other faith traditions and from other countries so that we may be continually engaged in the process of decolonizing ourselves and become postcolonial subjects in the process of reading other texts.

Postcolonial Asian feminist theologies and globalization

Such multi-logue across national, racial and religious boundaries is vital to the flourishing of grassroots social movements, including feminist movements, in our increasingly interconnected world. The old form of colonialism as territorial control has been superseded by neo-colonialism and domination in the neo-liberal market economy. The local and the global cannot be easily separated. Sociologist Roland Robertson has coined the term *glocalization* to describe the adaptation of worldwide processes to local situations. This applies not only to economic globalization, but also to cultural production and religious phenomena such as fundamentalism.

> In order to meet the challenges of the globalized world, postcolonial Asian feminist theologies cannot focus on a single nation, or on the Asian continent, without paying attention to how Asia is reshaping the world and how global forces constantly impact on the region. Thus, postcolonial Asian feminist theologies need to be transnational in scope and glocal in their focus.

Since the Cold War ended, the world has not enjoyed peace and stability. In many parts of Asia, ethnic, class and religious conflicts have taken place, causing bloodshed and wreaking havoc on society. Military juntas continue to exert enormous influence in a number of Asian countries. The road to democracy and political participation in postcolonial Asia remains long and tortuous. Marlene Perera, whose country Sri Lanka has been torn apart by decades of ethnic strife, has written on the impact of war and armed conflicts on the lives of women in Asia. Women become refugees, exiled from their homes and forced to live in precarious situations. As part of the struggle for peace and reconciliation, Perera calls for renewed commitment to interreligious dialogue and solidarity. Postcolonial Asian feminist theologians must probe deeper into the religious roots of violence, because much suffering has been inflicted in the name of the sacred. Religion has been mobilized to support nationalistic causes, define insiders and outsiders, and promote hatred and intolerance. We must challenge such misuses of religion, while at the same time looking for resources for compassion, tolerance and reconciliation in the rich Asian religious traditions. Working for peace and sustaining hope in dire conditions requires a spirituality that is inclusive, embodied and open to taking risks.

The work of postcolonial Asian feminist theologies is not done in Asia alone, but also by Asian feminists living in diaspora. In the USA there is the network of Pacific, Asia, and North American Asian Women in Theology and Ministry. Its members have met annually since 1985 to facilitate the development of Pacific Asian and North American Asian women's theologies. The network enables the cross-fertilization of ideas and conversations about gender, colonialism, racism and classism from more than one vantage point. The anthology *Off the Menu: Asian and Asian North American Women's Religion and Theology* contains essays that examine the Asia-Pacific region from transnational and postcolonial perspectives. The diasporic experience of some of the contributors opens new horizons for looking at national identity, citizenship and cultural authenticity and their relationship to religious and theological claims.

Conclusion

With the phenomenal rise of China and India and the economic growth of the newly industrialized nations on the Pacific Rim, Asia is poised to play a key role in global politics in the twenty-first century. Competition for resources and markets may lead to potential international conflicts and disputes. Already in the West, some people have argued that China is colonizing Africa, just as Europe did in the past. In the midst of Asia's rapid changes, postcolonial theory, with its astute analysis of imperial formation – old and new – will assist feminist theologians to gauge the present and envision the future. Some of the emerging Asian theologians and biblical scholars have expressed interest in the theory. I hope that they will make great contributions to the discourse in the near future.

SUGGESTED QUESTIONS

1 How do you understand the term postcolonial? What are the aims of postcolonial Asian feminist theologies?

2 How have women done theology in the Asian context? What issues relating to women are dealt with in postcolonial feminist theology in Asia?

3 Can postcolonial feminist theologies be relevant to your own contexts? Think of a situation where women in contexts that you are familiar with are trying to change their communities. How might feminist theology help them?

4 How might postcolonial feminist theology shed new light on reading the story of the Samaritan Woman at the Well found in John 4? You may like to answer this question by reflecting upon (a) how the woman's sexuality is controlled in this narrative, (b) how Jesus emerges as a revolutionary figure in this story and (c) the dialogue between cultures which takes place between Jesus, who is a Palestinian Jew, and the woman, who is a Samaritan.

6
From Orientalism to postcolonial: notes on reading practices

Rasiah S. Sugirtharajah

 **Abstract**

In this essay Sugirtharajah critically reviews three different modes of biblical interpretation in the Asian context, namely the Orientalist mode, the Anglican mode and the Nativistic mode, and proposes the necessity of a shift in Asian biblical hermeneutics towards what he calls a postcolonial reading or approach. He asserts that postcolonial interpretation will critique the universalizing and totalizing tendencies as well as the myth of objectivity of modernist European interpretations of the Bible and expose them as a means of control. Furthermore, it will recognize that a text contains multiple meanings. A postcolonial model of interpretation will recover the protest voices in the text from the perspectives of the marginalized and will also seek to read and hear the biblical narratives alongside other communally inspired sacred narratives, thus avoiding the totalitarian and totalizing claims of biblical narratives.

 Introduction

> A book of half lives, partial truths, conjecture, interpretations, and perhaps even some mistakes. What better homage to the past than to acknowledge it thus, rescue it and recreate it, without presumption of judgment, and as honestly, though perhaps as incompletely as we know ourselves, as part of the life of which we all are a part?
>
> At the end of it all, I too lie exposed to my own inquiry, also captive to the book.   M. G. Vasanji, *The Book of Secrets*, pp. 331–2

What I propose to do in this paper is to work out a possible mode of biblical interpretation for Asia that I will call postcolonial reading or a postcolonial approach. Of course the attempt to establish a postcolonial interpretation will have its application far beyond Asia. Before I explain what postcolonial criticism means, I should like to review briefly various interpretative options now available in Asia. Unlike the late Pol Pot, no one starts with a year zero, or for that matter with a clean slate. My current research interest is inevitably linked with earlier modes of interpretation. Surveying the Asian scene, I identify three modes of biblical interpretation with origins in the colonial era. These can be categorized as Orientalist, Anglicist and Nativist. As a future possibility, I would like to propose 'Postcolonialist' reading as a mode of interpretation.

We will define these modes as we go along. The fact that these categories are yoked to particular phases of the imperialist era and couched in colonial terminology is itself a reminder and an indication that the Bible was seen as an ineluctable instrument of the Empire. One of the devices employed to promote the Bible in India was to use, as propaganda, King George V's confession that he himself read the Bible every day. This enabled missionaries of the time to market the Bible as 'the book your Emperor reads' (Roe, 1965: 153).

The Orientalist mode: inventing tradition

Orientalism was the cultural policy advocated by colonialists as a way of promoting and reviving India's ancient linguistic, philosophical and religious heritage. This policy was instrumental in excavating India's rich cultural past and, in the process, introducing Indians to the glories of their ancient heritage. It also elevated the Sanskrit language to a venerated status, and ensured that learning the language was important to the natives. Orientalist policy was instigated partly out of the need to acquaint rulers with the native way of life, and partly as a way of effectively controlling and managing the Indian people. The Orientalist rejuvenation of Indian culture provided an enormous impetus to the development of biblical interpretation in India. The Indian converts of the nineteenth century, following the path set by their erstwhile Hindu colleagues, were involved in retrieving the neglected Indian classical texts rather than engaging with the Western classical tradition as the missionaries had expected. The 'natives' were not passive consumers of the past the Orientalists manufactured for them. The indigenous intelligence saw itself as an active interpreter between the past and the present, and busied itself selecting texts and narratives from the past to meet current national concerns.

In the writings of Krishna Mohan Banerjea (1813–85), a Bengali convert to the Christian faith, one sees the signs of Orientalism. He saw his task as showing the interconnections between the (Hindu) Vedic texts and biblical narratives. His intention was twofold. One, to show that the Vedas come closer to the spirit of Christianity than do the Hebrew scriptures; and two, to

49

demonstrate that the pristine, pure form of Hinduism found in the Vedas is identical with the Christian scriptures; thus identifying contemporary Indian Christians as the spiritual heirs of Aryan Hindus. Banerjea's engagement with Vedic texts and biblical narratives was the affirmation, endorsement and realization of the dream of the Orientalists – that Christian natives would one day encounter native Hindus with their own textual tradition.

The Orientalist construction of a Golden Age of Indian civilization based on ancient Sanskrit texts and Sanskritic criticism continues to inform and influence Indian Christian biblical interpretation. Like the earliest Orientalists, some of the current biblical interpreters, including both Indians and expatriates, see the recovery of Brahmanical tradition and the reintroduction of Sanskrit as a way of bringing to Indian Christians the truth of their own ancient tradition. The supreme examples of using ancient Indian texts to elucidate Christian interpretation appear in T. M. Manickam's *Dharma According to Manu and Moses* (1977) and R. H. S. Boyd's *Khristadvaita: A Theology for India* (1977) and Swami Abhishiktananda's labelling St John's Gospel a Christian *Upanishad* (Abhishiktananda, 1969: 85). While these interpreters were encouraging us to engage in comparative hermeneutics, Paul Gregorios (1979), Thomas Manickam (1982, 1984), Anand Amaladass (1979, 1990, 1994) and Sister Vandana (1989) were making proposals for borrowing critical tools from Sanskritic literary tradition to enhance Indian biblical hermeneutics as an alternative to the hegemonic Western strategies of interpretation. Gregorios urged Indians to recover the distinctive interpretative principles laid down by three Indian philosophical schools – the *Nyaya*, *Vaisesika* and *Sankhya* – while Manickam proposed a cross-cultural hermeneutics based on three Indian classical schools, *Mimamsa*, *Vyankarana* and the Vedantic school of *Sankara*, which had developed their own methods to understand revelation. The recent call by Anand Amaladass and Sister Vandana to revive the *dhvani* method of interpretation also falls within this Orientalist stream.

The Anglicist mode: the introduction of Western tools to shape the colonial 'other'

Anglicism arose as an ideological programme to counter Orientalism in colonial India. A pioneer in this was Alexander Duff, the Church of Scotland's first missionary to India. Anglicism was a strategic attempt to replace indigenous texts and learning with Western science and Western modes of thinking and to integrate the colonial into the culture of the colonizer. Translated eventually into biblical studies, Anglicism meant the introduction of Western modes of biblical investigation in Indian theological colleges. In practice, this meant two things: the importing of Western reading techniques in the form of historical criticism and its allied disciplines, and the ushering in of biblical theology with its grand themes, namely, the Bible as a theologically unified whole, the self-disclosure of God through historical events, the distinctive biblical mentality which differed from the mentality of its Hellenistic neighbours, and the unique features of biblical faith in contrast to the Near Eastern environment. Anglicism also brought with it the modernist ideas of belief in grand narratives, recognition of objective reality, and the view that narratives are objects with determinate meaning; hence, Anglicism brought modernism's commitment to discover *the* single/original meaning of the text.

A quick glance at any issue of the Indian biblical quarterly *Bible Bhashyam* will provide plenty of examples of creative Asian mimicry of Western interpretative methods. Interestingly, these methods are used not only by the hegemonic Asian theologies, but also by a variety of subaltern groups – Indian Dalits, Japanese Burakumins, Korean Minjung, indigenous people and Asian women – to amplify their voices.

The Nativistic mode: reinscribing vernacular traditions

Nativistic interpretation arose among those suffocating under the double burden of Western and Sanskritic theories, and who wanted to revive their own language traditions. Nativism is an attempt to animate *bhasa* or vernacular tradition. It prompted an awareness of the various non-Sanskritic traditions. Significantly, it has helped restore balance by offering an alternative classical culture in Tamil and has paved the way for a shift from a Vedantic to a bhakti type of religious experience. It has called into question the hegemonic status of Sanskrit and has opened up multiple performance and textual traditions. It is a hermeneutical enterprise which takes place within a specific cultural and language context and is bound by the rules set by that particular language and culture.

Nativism draws on both performance traditions and textual tradition. The nativistic biblical interpretations of Sadhu Sundar Singh (Punjabi), Mungamuri Devadas (Telugu), Vaman Tilak (Marathi) and H. A. Krishna Pillai (Tamil) borrow largely from the vernacular mode of storytelling. The works of H. A. Krishna Pillai and A. J. Appasamy fall within this category. While Krishna Pillai drew on his Vaishnavite tradition, Appasamy made use of both Vaishnavite and Saivite heritage and drew on bhakti insights to reread biblical texts.

At the risk of oversimplification, I have outlined here three interpretative models that are currently available. I would like to make clear that these do not supersede one another, but sit side by side and coexist. Because of the shortage of space this is not the occasion to evaluate these modes. However, in my proposal for a postcolonial criticism, you will note some of the weaknesses of these methods.

✳ Towards postcolonial criticism

Two critical categories which are at the centre of current hermeneutical discussion are *postmodernism* and *postcolonialism*. Needless to say, both are contested terms, and they have certain affinities. Nonetheless postmodernism is still seen as Eurocentric in its conceptual and aesthetic emphases. Though there are attempts to collapse postmodernism and postcolonialism into one and to erase their differences, postcolonialism is emerging as a distinctive discourse on its own. The recognition of postcolonialism as a branch of cultural studies and the rapid emergence of a supporting literature are evidence of this (Williams and Chrisman, 1993; Ashcroft, Griffiths and Tiffin, 1995; Mongia, 1996; Childs and Williams, 1997; and Moore-Gilbert, 1997).

I imagine that postcoloniality will be the arena in which future biblical interpretation in India, or for that matter in Asia, will be worked out.

> Postcolonial biblical interpretation is the interpretation which will emerge from people who once were colonized by European powers (or, in the case of Korea, by imperial Japan) but who now have some political freedom, while continuing to live with burdens from the past and experiencing forms of economic and cultural neocolonialism.

This form of interpretation will emerge from the social, economic and cultural margins, which will be seen as 'sites of survival', 'fighting grounds' and 'sites for pilgrimage' (Minh-ha, 1991: 17). It will emerge among nations, communities and groups which have been victims of the old imperialism and are now victims of the current globalization, and who have been kept away from power only to achieve an identity nurtured and nourished by their own goals and aspirations.

Postcolonial interpretation will be a way of critiquing the universalist, totalizing forms of European interpretation. What will distinguish postcolonial reading from Orientalist and Anglicist modes of interpretation is the conviction that the modernist values they espoused, such as objectivity and neutrality, are expressions of political, religious and scholarly power.

> Postcolonial interpretation will reject the myth of objective or neutral truth and will replace it with a perception of truth as mapped, constructed and negotiated.

Postcolonial criticism recognizes that interpreters have to be freed from traditional interpretative powers so that the voice of the voiceless may be heard. Such freedom will be manifest in what Fanon calls 'fighting literature', 'a revolutionary literature' (Fanon, 1990: 179), the authentic expression of people tired of the exasperating attempts to assimilate and mimic the hegemonic Orientalist and Anglicist modes of interpretation. It will recognize the value of the hidden or occluded accounts of numerous groups – women, minorities, the disadvantaged and the displaced.

Unlike the Orientalist, Anglicist and Nativist modes, postcolonial criticism will not engage in recovering the single meaning of the text, but will recognize a multiplicity of meanings.

The retrieval and reinscription of the past becomes a crucial hermeneutical activity. But unlike the Orientalist, Anglicist and Nativist approaches, postcolonial reading will negotiate the past differently, 'not as a static fetishized phase to be literally reproduced, but as fragmented sets of narrated memories and experiences on the basis of which to mobilize contemporary communities' (Shohat, 1992: 109).

There are at least two marks of postcolonial criticism. One will take its cue from the cultural critic Stuart Hall and look for what he calls oppositional or protest voices in the texts. Hall identifies four codes embodied in current discourse on television – hegemonic, professional, negotiated, and protest or oppositional (Hall, 1973: 16–19). Biblical texts reflect all four codes. Traditional interpretations generally fraternize with the first three. Postcolonialism, in contrast, will look for protesting or oppositional voices in the texts. For instance, in the parable of the tenants (Mark 12.1–11; Matt. 21.33–43; Luke 20.9–18), commentators often invest this story with allegorical meanings or look for allusions to the Hebrew Bible. It is usually read either from an overly Christological perspective or from the property owner's perspective. Rarely is the parable read from the point of view of the people in the audience. Most commentators erase the role of the people from the parable. There is no need for me to rehearse it. When one by one the tenants kill the messengers, the householder finally sends his son, who is also killed by them. 'What will the owner do?' asks Jesus, and goes on to say that he will destroy those tenants and give the vineyard to others.

This parable occurs in Mark, Matthew and Luke. Unlike the other two accounts, in Luke this parable is specifically told to the people, who come out with an interesting reaction. When they hear that the owner is going to destroy the tenants and give the land to others, the people's response is 'God forbid' (Luke 20.16b, AV). They express shock, for they are the heirs of Yahweh's allotment of land, which has been stolen from them. The audience knows that once the land is gone they not only will lose their income but will also be at the mercy of the new owner's working arrangements.

> What postcolonial criticism will do is to bring to the front marginal and often neglected elements in the texts and, in the process, subvert the traditional meaning.

Many narratives and voices have been forgotten by institutions and by conventional exegesis. Postcolonial criticism will carry out an exegesis that digs down to neglected meanings, as a way of commemorating such voices.

The other mark of postcolonial reading will be to advocate a wider hermeneutical agenda which will place the study of sacred texts – Christian-Hindu, Christian-Buddhist, Christian-Confucian – within the intersecting histories which constitute them.

> Postcolonial interpretation will replace the totalitarian and totalizing claims of biblical narratives with the claim that they have to be understood as the negotiated narrative strategies of a community and to be read and heard along with other communally inspired sacred narratives.

A postcolonial reading will see these texts within an intertextual continuum, embodying a multiplicity of perspectives. This will mean looking for the hermeneutical relations that these texts imply and inspire, and resisting any attempts to subsume one relationship under the other. The issue for us is how these diverse texts can help us account for our collective identities. The recent study of Matthew's missionary command read alongside the Buddhist *Mahavagga* text by George Soares-Prabhu comes close to the postcolonial intertextual engagement I have in mind (Soares-Prabhu, 1994). In this article the 'Other' is celebrated without insisting on the protocols set by missionary apologetics. Let me underline this last point with an anecdote. This comes from *Gora*, a novel by Rabindranath Tagore written during colonial days. It is a story about the spiritual journey of the hero of the novel, Gora, which takes him to a fanatical belief in Vedic Hinduism as a panacea for India's ills, and on from that to his enlightenment, which comes through his foster mother, Sucharita. After his enlightenment he is in search of a new identity. He says,

> Today I am really an Indian. In me is no longer any opposition between Hindu, Mussalman and Christian. Today every caste in India is my caste, food of all is my food . . . all these days I have been carrying about with me an unseen gulf of separation which I have never been able to cross over! Therefore in my mind there was a kind of void, which I tried by various devices to ignore. I tried to make that emptiness look more beautiful by decorating it with all kinds of artistic work . . . Now that I have been delivered from those fruitless attempts at inventing such useless décor I feel that I am alive again.
>
> (Tagore, 1989 [1924]: 406)

Then he goes on to ask for 'the *mantram* of that deity who belongs to all, Hindu, Mussalman, Christian and Brahmo alike – the doors to whose temple are never closed to any person of any caste whatever' (Tagore, 1989 [1924]: 407). In a postcolonial context, Gora would agree that what we need is not just a *mantram*, a sacred word, but many *mantrams* which are manifestly pluralistic and validated by many communities.

At a time when people are thrown together and live in multilingual, multiracial and multifaith societies, the question is how a people can affirm their language, take pride in their race, be fervent about their faith, cherish their ethnicity and celebrate their differences, and at the same time share the land, its water and its fruits with others who also make claims about their language, ethnicity, religion and culture. The task before us is not so much to celebrate the new hybridized identity or to marvel at the way we have used the right jargon as a posture and power play, but to help in addressing the questions which affect people's lives. The worth and the credibility of postcolonial criticism will be judged by how it orchestrates the unique and fragile and imagined claims of one community against another.

 SUGGESTED QUESTIONS

1 What are the three different modes of biblical interpretation that prevail in the Asian context and have colonial origins?

2 What does looking for multiple meanings in the text imply? How can one look for multiple meanings in the text?

3 What would be the main features of a postcolonial reading of the Bible?

4 What, according to the cultural critic Stuart Hall, are the four codes that are present in current discourses? What happens when one pays attention to the protest voices in the text?

7
Postcolonialism and Hong Kong Christianity

Wai Ching Angela Wong

 Abstract

Wong traces the development of Christianity in Hong Kong from a postcolonial perspective, bringing out the complex nature of the relationship between the colonizer and the colonized. She explores the beneficial social, economic and political dimensions of the alliance between colonial rule and church development before the handing over of Hong Kong to China in 1997 which posed challenges for Hong Kong Christians' embracing of a Chinese identity. The identity crisis (where Hong Kong Christians were caught between three identities, namely Hong Konger, national Chinese and Christian) which immediately preceded the handover and continued after it, presented Christianity in Hong Kong with unprecedented challenges. Christianity in Hong Kong was caught in a tension arising between identification with the local (Hong Kong) and the national (Chinese) and between Chinese cultural and Western religious demands. This, according to Wong, has resulted in a condition of 'no-return' for postcolonial Hong Kong Christians.

 Introduction

Postcolonialism is often understood to imply a political involvement in resistance to colonial rule over the land of a native people. It is sometimes immediately equivalent to anti-colonial politics, including nationalistic movements toward political independence. The prefix 'post' is therefore taken to refer not so much to a particular historical period but to the ideologies and practices of resistance by the native people against their foreign rulers. In much Western postcolonial theological literature, the term is applied largely in the sense of anti-imperialism, the battle against a legacy of Eurocentric theologies which imposes its universal claims over Christians of non-Western cultures and histories. In this sense, postcolonialism has served as a significant intellectual tool for the critical appropriation of the Diaspora theologians in their theologizing work in the West. As it demonstrates, postcolonialism has served a discursive function of reclaiming the voice of the minorities on the margin over against the dominant power of the centre in the identity politics of the West. However, a critical analysis and appreciation of postcoloniality in its various contexts and concrete historicity generate a very different understanding of the political relationships between the colonizers and the colonized in the case of Christianity in Hong Kong.

The colonial beginning

Often referred to as a small fishing town before colonial occupation, Hong Kong caught the world's attention in 1997 as one of the last Western colonies to be returned to its motherland. Its history before 1841, when Hong Kong Island was ceded to Britain under the unequal treaty of Nanking, was almost unknown, and so seems to have been interwoven for ever with colonialism and its legacy.

Before Britain took over, the island's population was only about 2,000, largely fishermen and Hakka farmers. Soon after 1842, with the transport of people and goods on and off the harbour, the role of Hong Kong as a trading port was gradually established. The population slowly increased during the 1840s, mainly as a result of the numbers of coolies, servants, rock-miners and merchants, not to mention pirates, criminals, triad members and opium traders, who lived around the increasingly busy port – those who the missionaries considered 'with few exceptions' as people of 'the lowest description and character' (Smith, 1847: 76). On the other hand, while the British Steamship Company operated ocean liners between the mainland and Hong Kong, and between Europe and the Far East, a few Chinese fleets had been slowly developing their own business in competition. The latter formed the basis of the main Chinese business sector that enabled the later economic development of Hong Kong. The establishment of a strong trade network between Europe and South-East Asia and Australia was therefore firmly founded in the colony's early years. In short, the location of Hong Kong, with China as its hinterland and its connection to the world through its harbour, established the role of the territory from the very beginning.

Many missionary churches began to move into Hong Kong, their way eased by the British colonial government. The Revd I. J. Roberts, an American Baptist, moved from Macau in 1842, while the Revd James Legge, the chief representative of the London Missionary Society, came to the island from Malacca in 1843 and was instrumental in founding its British colonial educational system. The first Anglican colonial chaplain, the Revd Vincent J.

Stanton, came from Macau in the same year, his primary task being to serve the local British community; a Chinese Anglican church – named Chung Hua Sheng Kung Hui (The Anglican Church in China) was set up only in 1912. The American Board (ABCFM) and the American Lutherans also came during the same period. In 1847 French priests were the first Catholic missionaries to arrive in Hong Kong, with the first vicariate established in 1874. The topography of the missionary enterprise in Hong Kong had largely taken shape by then.

> Because of the historically cooperative relationship between Church and state in England, the churches in Hong Kong, especially the Anglican and Roman Catholic Churches, enjoyed extensive privileges and influence in the community.

In other words, from the 1840s until 1997 the mainland churches were a part of the colonial establishment. Intensive collaboration in social development between the government and the churches began when a massive influx of mainland refugees arrived after the expulsion of missionaries from China in the 1950s. The acute need for welfare and education and the availability of Christian personnel during this time provided the churches with an ideal opportunity to assert their influence. Alongside the Hong Kong Chinese Christian Churches Union, formed in 1915 to coordinate evangelical work and social services, the Hong Kong Christian Council was established in 1954 to minister to the social needs of the growing numbers of immigrants from the mainland and to coordinate emergency relief. In the late 1960s, when the British-Hong Kong government was under great pressure to cope with escalating resentment of colonialism, instigated by the surge of political activity on the mainland, a system of social welfare services was put in place primarily with the support of the churches. In consequence, by the time of the handover in the 1990s, Christian operation in the three sectors of education, medicine and social services accounted for 40 per cent, 30 per cent and 60 per cent respectively of action in the community. There are thus only a few people in Hong Kong whose lives have not been touched by Christianity in some way; evangelism in Hong Kong has taken full advantage of its opportunities with the various aspects of social development in the territory.

A closer look shows that the impact of the alliance between colonial governance and church development is not only social but economic and political. The proportion of Christians in Hong Kong, at about 10 per cent of the population, is believed to be the third highest in Asia, smaller only than the Philippines and South Korea. The largest growth has taken place within the free independent churches, such as the Baptist churches, the Evangelical Free Church of China and the China Missionary Alliance. These evangelical churches have been fast catching up with the mainstream churches in their share of managing Hong Kong schools and social services; in addition they have organized regular evangelical campaigns that aggressively promote the Christian faith through a range of publications and, in order to appeal to the younger generation, via the media. Together, the mainstream and evangelical free churches of Hong Kong have successfully produced the most educated and professional sector of the island's population, maximizing the protection and privileges afforded by British colonialism.

In the first public report of church statistics, conducted by the Hong Kong Church Renewal Movement in December 1999, members of the Hong Kong churches were characterized as middle class, with many professionals, and generally well-educated; 58.9 per cent of Protestants and 57 per cent of Catholics described themselves as middle or upper middle class, compared to 41.8 per cent of those with no religious allegiance (Pavey, 2005). Moreover, 33 per cent of the Christian population received tertiary education as compared to only 17.5 per cent of the general population. And a 1995 survey showed that 40.9 per cent of the general population who had attained a postgraduate degree were Christians. In terms of vocation, 34 per cent of the church population consists of professionals, while the figure for the general population is 21 per cent. These outcomes are clearly a result of the distinctive status of Christian schools in the colony. According to Kwok Nai Wang, former general secretary of successively the Hong Kong Christian Council and the Hong Kong Christian Institute, 25 of the 30 most famous secondary schools were run by the churches in the 1950s and they almost entirely monopolized admission into the University of Hong Kong until the 1960s. Since the University of Hong Kong remained the island's only university until 1963, it is not surprising to find that its graduates still constitute the core of Hong Kong's elite. Today, about 75 per cent of the top administrative personnel in the Special Administrative Region government are Christians, an unusually high figure considering that only about 9.6 per cent of the general population are Christians.

> Because of the privileged position that Christians have occupied in the government, legislature, education and other professional fields since the colonial years, the influence of Christianity in Hong Kong cannot be overestimated.

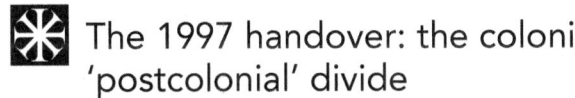

The 1997 handover: the colonial and 'postcolonial' divide

If, since 1842, the growth of Christianity had gone hand in hand with British colonial rule, 1997 presented an unprecedented challenge to Hong Kong's churches. The decade leading to Britain's handover of Hong Kong to China had been a period of intense 'soul-searching', especially for Christians. The island's people were confronted with the question of identity, with the result that a sense of unique 'Hong Kong-ness', as opposed to 'Chineseness', emerged. A gradual transition in people's consciousness developed, from the migrant's sense of 'borrowed place, borrowed time' to that of the first established generation's sense of 'my land, my people'. One apparent phenomenon was the blossoming of creativity related to the use of Cantonese, the mother tongue of the majority Hong Kong people, in cinema, art, literature and popular culture. This sense of a local identity intensified as the community witnessed through eyewitness accounts as well as the media the Chinese military crackdown following the Tiananmen student demonstration in 1989. Hong Kong Christianity, born as an imported religion and culture and yet rooted in the territory for a hundred years, suddenly found itself faced with a cultural and political dilemma.

When China first opened up in the early 1980s, persecution of Chinese church leaders under the Cultural Revolution had been the main story related by the mainland Chinese Christian community to their first visitors. The inherent ideological conflict between Communism and Christianity was immediately recalled. There had been doubts as to the existence of religious freedom in China even before the 4 June massacre in Tiananmen Square and that day's events gave a major cultural and political shock to the Christian community in the years immediately following. The handover of Hong Kong to China was associated with threats, hostility and distrust, especially in the evangelical churches, which had been particularly sympathetic to the underground churches of the mainland.

In order to safeguard the faith of the general Christian community and to declare solidarity with the population at large, the Hong Kong Christian Council and other Christian organizations held a series of seminars in the 1980s reflecting on and reaffirming their commitment to the future and destiny of Hong Kong. In 1984, 'A Christian Faith Statement in View of the Present Social and Political Changes in Hong Kong' was produced and signed by more than 60 pastors, confessing their faith in God, their persistence in mission, their commitment to social and national responsibility, and their devotion to the renewal of church and ecumenical witness. In August the same year, more than 200 denominational churches and evangelistic organizations jointly signed another document, 'The Declaration of Religious Freedom', demanding the preservation of freedom of evangelism, religious gatherings, and permission to continue conducting social services. In September, 21 senior Hong Kong Christian leaders took the two documents with them to a meeting with officials in Beijing in order to register their concerns. Despite these efforts, however, the high emigration rate of Christians could not be reversed. Compared to the general population, of whom one in eight people emigrated in the 1990s, the figure for the Christian community was one in four. And the emigration ratio of Hong Kong pastors aged 30 to 50 between 1985 and 1993 was three in four.

Rather than welcoming decolonization and returning to their mother country, Hong Kong Christians were caught in a dilemma whereby, as a result of the handover, they were forgoing colonial protection and returning to a sovereign country which opposed Christianity ideologically and historically.

> In the years immediately before 1997, Christians were placed in a seemingly impossible situation of partaking in three identities – Hong Konger, national Chinese and Christian – which did not always sit comfortably with one another. Whether they chose one or another of these identities, for Hong Kong Chinese Christians this meant a degree of hybridity – they could never feel 'pure' in any one nature.

Suspicion among any one of the three parties regarding Christians' double or triple loyalties remains forever with them. For politically conservative churches, the practical option is to maintain a low profile in national matters so as not to jeopardize their future. For progressive Christians, their mission is to stretch their complex identities to their broadest possible limits, living all three aspects of their identities in tension and, in the hope of bringing about a better China, participating actively in the democratic movement of Hong Kong. The first approach readily seeks the pro-establishment path and submits to a hardly mature Hong Kong identity under the 'neo-colonial' identity of patriotic national Chinese. The second attempts to sustain a form of postcolonial resistance and challenges the local establishment for their easy submission to the political authority of Beijing.

Living between colonizers and Hong Kong postcolonialism

Rey Chow's representative essay, 'Between Colonizers: Hong Kong's Postcolonial Self-writing in the 1990s' (1992), describes very well the situation faced by Hong Kong people who remained in the territory after 1997. Her argument presents Hong Kong as a city that was handed over by one colonizer to another. In the name of the sovereign country, under the pretence of 'one country two systems', the new colonizer rules Hong Kong from the political centre in the north. China and Hong Kong have been developing entirely different social, economic and political systems over the past hundred years and there has been very little substance to sustain their supposedly common cultural roots. What is worse, family blood ties between the earlier Chinese settlers in Hong Kong and their relatives in their home villages were almost completely cut off due to continual political change and turmoil on the mainland between the 1950s and the 1970s. When the door of China was reopened in the 1980s its economic condition was miserable and its political reforms shattered. In contrast, Hong Kong people found their colonial experience not entirely one of exploitation but, for many, something of 'a blessing in disguise'. At the point of return to China, not only were the Hong Kong elites nostalgic for 'the good old days' but also the general population, who found themselves much better off both socially and economically than their home villagers. Rather than happily celebrating the return of sovereignty to the people, most of the population before 1997 felt resentful that Hong Kong was being handed over yet to another 'foreign' power, one which was Communist, autocratic and economically backward.

> The idea of equating the mother country with a new 'colonizer' would sound blasphemous to many but is not inappropriate in the case of Hong Kong.

Postcolonialism in Hong Kong is therefore never a straightforward case of resisting the political dominance of a foreign power from abroad. The strategic significance of Hong Kong in its situation between Chinese Communism and British colonialism for almost a century has produced a place and a people full of ambiguities. Both its former British colonizer and its reclaimed Communist mother country have found in such a historical accident much benefit for their respective development before and after 1997. This also means that this place has remained under the close control of its masters – first the British and then the Chinese in Beijing. Interestingly, because of Hong Kong's unique location between China and the Western world, its people have continued to play the role of 'middlemen', a role Carl Smith first highlighted in the context of the early colonial period:

> [The colonizer] created a [hu]man who stood between two cultures, a man who was not altogether at home in either. He was not wholly in the Chinese Model, nor was he altogether Western. This dual aspect of his thought and outlook enabled him to fill a needed place in the meeting of the Chinese nation with foreigners promoting trade and commerce. The foreign merchant needed a Chinese to supervise the Chinese side of his business. Chinese merchants trading with foreigners needed a Chinese who understood the foreigner and who could speak his language. The Governments of both China and Hong Kong needed translators and interpreters . . . This group of Chinese interpreters, compradors, advisors to officials and Government, and men in various professions created a distinct culture in the China coast cities.   (Smith, 1985: 10–11)

Rather than a transformed politics in accordance with the dictum of 'Hong Kong people governing Hong Kong', the structure of governance remained 'colonial' in that the real ruling power continued to reside outside Hong

Kong. Postcolonialism in Hong Kong embraces fully Homi Bhabha's provocative strategy of hybridity, engaging at once modernity and tradition, and between the rule of law of its Western colonial master and the political contingency of 'feeling the rocks while crossing the river' of the Chinese nation. In a vivid description of the city, Xi Xi – a writer born in China, living mostly in Hong Kong and famous in Taiwan – depicts the people of Hong Kong as having only *chengxi* (the identity of a city) but not *guoxi* (the identity of a nation), and being forced to write in a language (Mandarin Chinese) that is different from our mother tongue (Cantonese). Unlike independence movements in many Asian countries, Hong Kong has to engage in a postcolonial politics which has always to retain a critical distance from state nationalism.

> In the same vein, rather than joining the general theological engagement in Asia with the upholding of national identity and culture, Christianity in Hong Kong has to face the tension arising between identification with the local and the national, and between Chinese cultural and Western religious traditions.

Instead of achieving resolution of the divided conscience of the colonized and being able to celebrate a renewed national identity, Christians in Hong Kong must juggle their triple identities of Hong Konger, Chinese and Christian, and maintain a balance between anxiety over freedom of religion and negotiation with the Communist designation of religion's role and place in Chinese society. In short, Christianity in Hong Kong complicates the 'post' of postcolonialism in that it includes not only the politics of resistance but also accommodation and negotiation with the legacy that started with colonialism and continued in a different form thereafter. The condition of postcolonial Christians is one of 'no-return'; it is a conversion into an identity that is self-contradictory at its root and that lies at the crossroads of an imported culture and political legacy and an alienated nativity. The battle of postcolonial Christians is therefore not so much about fighting an external enemy in the colonizer, but the internal conflicts and splits imprinted for all time by the power of domination.

 SUGGESTED QUESTIONS

1 Briefly explain the colonial history of Hong Kong. What were the dilemmas faced by Hong Kong Christians following the independence of Hong Kong?

2 What was the impact of the alliance between colonial governance and church development on the social and economic life of Hong Kong?

3 What was the impact of colonialism on the identity of the people?

4 Using bullet points or brief notes, outline important historical events in your town/region or country. Plot changes in society, politics and economics alongside those points. Now add changes to cultural trends and religious movements. What involvement does the Church have in these changes? What involvement do you think it should have? Do the explanations of postcolonial theology here and in other chapters help you answer this question?

8
Asian Christologies: a postcolonial reconstruction

C. I. David Joy

 Abstract

Joy gives a broad overview of the arrival of Christianity in Asia, paying particular attention to the history of Christianity in the Indian context, from the debatable St Thomas tradition to the development of the Church of South India in 1947. He points to similar histories in other Asian countries like China, Taiwan, Korea and Japan which have foregrounded the consequent development of diverse streams of Asian Christology. He goes on to present the multiple faces of Asian Christologies, paying attention to liberation Christology, which was shaped in considerable part by Marxist thought; subaltern Christologies, which used sociological tools and addressed contextual issues; and postcolonial Christologies.

 Introduction

Passion and enthusiasm in academic study and research on Jesus of Nazareth has largely been sustained in Asia because the identity of Jesus has been linked with the identity of the researchers. Christology in the Asian context involves not only dealing with the study and understanding of Jesus of Nazareth, with the help of canonical and non-canonical materials, but also re-presenting Christ in the light of the hopes and agonies of his followers, paying particular attention to their socio-political situations and experiences. This article is an attempt to provide a broad overview of Asian Christologies and highlight briefly some of their major forms.

 Defining Asian Christology

The origin and development of Asian Christology cannot be discussed without a proper understanding of Christianity in Asia. The history of Christianity in Asia began in the first century CE as some of the disciples of Jesus travelled to various parts of the continent which lay beyond the Roman Empire in order to preach the good news. Christian communities were subsequently formed in many places; for instance, it is believed that the Apostle Thomas came to India and established churches there. The relationship between the Roman Empire and India paved the way for the arrival of representatives of the Jesus movement/early Church at the beginning of the second century CE.

There is clear mention in the Acts of Thomas of the coming of Thomas as an apostle to India, although there are a number of questions still active among historians about the validity of this claim. However, Christian presence has been identified in various ways in the south Indian state of Kerala from the very early stages of the formation of Christianity.

This tradition continued in various forms. For instance, it can be seen in the visit of Bishop Dudi of Basra in 295–300 CE and in that of Pantaenus to India. It can also be seen in stone cross inscriptions of the sixth and seventh centuries CE (Kuriakose, 1982: 5–9). A. M. Mundadan, a church historian from India, makes the following comment on the St Thomas tradition:

> This romantic account is probably based on a historical nucleus, representing the first and second century oral tradition. From the fourth century on there is unanimity among Churches about the tradition. It is likely that this tradition has a double, independent origin . . . St Thomas the apostle preached the Gospel in South India and the origin of Indian Christians, at least initially, is to be attributed to this preaching. (Mundadan, 1984: 60-1)

Christian communities in India may be divided into those predating and those following the sixteenth century, when the arrival of the Portuguese made such a tremendous impact on their ecclesiology. According to Mundadan, between 1292 and 1293 the Franciscan missionary John of Monte Corvino, along with Nicolas de Pistoia, visited India and their visit can be regarded as part of the Latin mission of the Middle Ages. The arrival in 1498 of Vasco da Gama in Kerala brought the Portuguese to India. A few centuries later the British came to India for trade through the East India Company.

Till the end of the eighteenth century, no missionary work was carried out in India by the Church of England, although the Lutherans and the Roman Catholics were involved in such activity. In 1813, a bishopric was established in Calcutta and eventually many missionaries arrived. According to Stephen Neill, the governments of India and England made the governance of the church complex by introducing the Constitution, Canons and Rules of the Church of India, Burma and Ceylon (Neill, 1948). This complexity was further exacerbated by the presence of different 'levels' of ministers such as missionaries, chaplains and Indian pastors.

By about 1850, missionaries from different parts of India had begun to come together to strengthen their work and to achieve better co-ordination, leading to the formation of the South India United Church. Bishop Gell and Canon Sell thereafter introduced the system of Church Councils, which propelled the growth of evangelical Anglicanism in South India. Finally, on 27 September 1947, at St George's Cathedral, Madras, the Church of South India was formed when Bishop Jacob announced the coming together of the Madras, Travencore and Cochin, Tinnevelly and Dornakal Dioceses of the Church of India, Burma and Ceylon; the Madras, Madura, Malabar, Jaffna, Kannada, Telugu and Travencore Church Councils of the South India United Church; and the Methodist Church in South India, comprising the Madras, Trichinopoly, Hyderabad and Mysore Districts (Sundkler, 1965: 343). This process encouraged the native leadership to be active in understanding and defining the Christian faith from their own viewpoint, leading to the formation of the initial forms of native Christologies.

There are similar histories in China, Taiwan, Korea, Japan and other countries; as Kenneth Scott Latourette claims, Christianity 'was carried eastward and early in the seventh century was planted in China' (Latourette, 1953: 272). Latourette offers, with clear evidence, an account of the growth of Christianity in Japan, explaining that, after Francis Xavier initially spread the gospel in 1549, within a short span of time a number of churches had emerged.

In all these places Christianity had to engage with the native religions and cultures, mainly Buddhism. Therefore, we can be certain that the Christology developed during the period was a result of indigenization or inculturation. Since this reality remains a strong challenge in redefining Christology, we should note that in Asia there are many Christological streams.

Asian Christologies

> Asian Christologies have multiple faces. The multi-faceted nature of Asian Christologies is mainly due to the emergence of various contextual theologies in Asia.

In this process of articulating contextual theologies, certain main concepts within the native cultures were taken into consideration when determining the boundaries and shape of contextual expressions of the Christian faith, including the form of the Asian Jesus (Phan, 1996: 399).

A number of attempts have been made in the recent past to categorize Asian Christological thinking with the help of contextual theology. For instance, at the global level, three monographs – Robert J. Schreiter's *Faces of Jesus in Africa* (1991), R. S. Sugirtharajah's *Asian Faces of Jesus* (1993) and Volker Kuster's *The Many Faces of Jesus Christ* (1999) – have challenged the traditional Christological frameworks. All these books were widely discussed by academicians and pastoral leaders worldwide (Joy, 2007: 139), and were well received by readers seeking a different language from those traditionally used to understand the event of incarnation.

In the same way, Kwok Pui-lan in her book *Postcolonial Imagination and Feminist Theology* (2006) makes a stunning observation, from a feminist perspective, about the contextualization of Jesus Christ outside America and Europe. She states:

> But when we look outside of white America and Europe, we discern an interesting phenomenon, in that women in the Third World and in racial minority communities have not been preoccupied with the maleness of Christ as an issue. It is important to bear in mind that some of them have come from cultures that do not construct gender in a fixed and binary way, and they have ... proceeded to destabilize the gender of Christ and experiment with a dazzling array of new images – from Jesus as the Feminine Shakti to the bi/Christ! In the process, they have collectively turned the blue-eyed, middle-class, and sexually restrained Aryan Christ – a projection of white men in their own images – upside down. (Kwok Pui-lan, 2006: 25)

Kwok Pui-lan's articulation is a mix of cultural studies and gender studies. At the same time, it is a way of looking at ongoing trends in Christology with the help of history and politics. Since the name of Christ is hugely significant for the liberation struggles of people at the margins and peripheries, it is important to visit, revisit, conceptualize and reconceptualize the image of Jesus Christ with the help of contemporary studies.

In the sections that follow I briefly highlight some basic Christological streams in Asia. I am aware that these streams can be analysed in the light of the colonial milieu that prevailed in some Asian countries and the influence of modernism and postmodernism in the contextualization of Christology. However, since a detailed study of all the available fields is a Himalayan task, it is proposed to limit the discussion to a few representative examples.

Liberation Christology

With the introduction of Marxian ideology into the process of reading the Bible, many biblical interpreters began to use insights from liberation theology, which originated in the military context of Latin America and later came to Asia. Unlike other contextual theological ideas, this theology considered the strategy of resistance as a pattern of hope. There is no unified approach in presenting the image of Jesus Christ to be seen in the writings of liberation theologians. For instance,

> the works of the liberation theologians in the Asian context employ a rainbow of images in their presentations, such as Jesus with Asian culture and cross (C. S. Song), the contextual Jesus (Tissa Balasurya), Jesus with the Justice of God (Samuel Rayan), Jesus among the alienated ones (H. M. Katoppo), and Jesus and Minjung (Kim Yong-Bok).

Since several images of and reflections on Jesus can be found in liberation Christologies, I will only explain one example. Sebastian Kappen, from India, used the insights of liberation theology in order to re-present Jesus with a relevant meaning in the Indian context. Kappen's attempts to engage the Jesus tradition with some positive insights of Marxism could be considered as the foundation for the emergence of liberation theology in Asia. By taking liberation hermeneutics seriously, Kappen viewed the entry of modern Christianity 'as a colonial extension of the Church in Europe' (Kappen, 2003).

Kappen was able to propose a clear starting point for the Indian interpretation of the Bible: 'Christ – the counter culture'. This understanding makes the place of Jesus in liberation theology very significant, encouraging readers to recognize the liberative aspects of his life and ministry in Nazareth and accept them as models of Christian faith engagement (Kappen, 1977: 45).

> Liberation Christology in Asia is derived from bringing together the Jesus of the Gospels and the living experiences of people in different socio-political contexts within Asia.

In short, liberation Christology presents Jesus of Nazareth as the epicentre of Christology, drawing connections with ideas of the kingdom and the redemptive framework of God. Jesus Christ is always with the people in their situations of conflict, struggle and oppression (Joy, 2007: 138).

 ## Subaltern Christology

In the postcolonial context, those who suffer any kind of oppression at the hands of dominant and powerful groups are subalterns. Anthony Kolenchery in his article 'South Indian Contribution to Subaltern Alternative Theologies' defines the term subalterns as follows:

> The word 'subaltern' indicates a work of a lower order. It is the general articulation of 'subordination' in South Asian society expressed in terms of class, caste, creed, age or gender. Subaltern groups are often subject to the domination of the ruling class even when they rebel or protest. (Kolenchery, 2003: 125)

With the introduction of sociological methods to biblical interpretation by liberation theologians in Asia, a process of contextualization of theology and hermeneutics was initiated in the 1970s. This subsequently led to the development of subaltern Christologies. The process of native hermeneutics which preceded subaltern hermeneutics and sought to connect native traditions with the Christian story, was interesting but vague, as it did not address the real issues of the postcolonial context such as caste and culture. In such a context Saral K. Chatterji, who was Director of the Christian

Institute for the Study of Religion and Society (CISRS) in India, pioneered efforts towards a relevant expression of theology, which he called 'People's Theology'. People's theology encouraged oppressed communities to produce ground-breaking studies of the Bible and expressions of radical alternatives for human living which questioned the prevailing economic inequalities and caste-based exploitation. Chatterji summarizes the theological dimension of people's theology in the following manner: 'The other dimension of a people's theology can be summed up as the universal love of God in the particularity of Jesus' life, death and resurrection. The eschatological view of God's unifying love is possible because of the particularity of Jesus' (Chatterji, 1980: 23).

This affirmation eventually became a cornerstone for subaltern biblical hermeneutics and subaltern Christologies. Among the people's theologians in postcolonial India, Arvind P. Nirmal and Felix Wilfred have a special place as they made their own distinct contributions to subaltern theologies. Nirmal was the initiator of Dalit theology/Christology and Wilfred offered clear guidelines for subaltern Christology through a careful and systematic analysis of the postcolonial situation.

The emergence of Dalit Christology in the Indian context is an important trend, as it is clearly a pointer towards the future discourse of liberative Christology. A working definition of Dalit Christology is useful at this point. Dalits are the people who are considered to fall outside the caste system. In other words, they are 'no-people', who have no economic, cultural or political status in the eyes of the dominant groups (for more on Dalits and Dalit theology, see Chapter 15 of this volume, 'The "untouched" touching theology'). Though they were known as the fifth caste (*panchamas*) and were also called *Harijans* by Gandhi, literally meaning 'the children of God' (a term they considered offensive because it carried connotations of questionable paternity and illegitimacy), later they opted to call themselves Dalits.

According to Dalit theologian James Massey the root meaning of the term 'Dal' in Hebrew and Sanskrit is 'poor'. Therefore, Dalit theology is a search by the poor for their identity, and for recognition and meaning. This fundamental focus of Dalit theology is also the springboard for Dalit hermeneutics. Arvind P. Nirmal proposes the Christological aspect of Dalit hermeneutics and Dalit theology as follows:

> It is thus the humanity of Christ that makes the human ideological quest possible. We may also refer here to our understanding of the Incarnation. 'The Word became flesh' is how we understand the incarnation. It is when the Word becomes flesh and becomes a concrete historical existence that we can speak meaningfully of the incarnation. It is when the Word assumes and passes through all the stages of humanity redeeming it and renewing it that we have the incarnating process set in motion by God. (Nirmal, 1990: 34)

In a similar vein, the biblical scholar Dhyanchand Carr proposes an image of God for the liberation of the marginalized, focusing on 'God's chosen vulnerability; God's partnership in suffering and the redemptive purpose of unjust suffering' (Carr, 2002: 67).

Felix Wilfred and some others have used the expression subaltern Christology to present their hermeneutical deliberations in a postcolonial situation.

> Subaltern Christology aims to highlight the vision of Christ, and urges the followers of Christ to try to transcend the frontiers of ethnicity, tribalism, nationalism and so on and move towards a just and egalitarian society (Wilfred, 1999: vii).

To get over these fundamental frontiers is a long process. And it is important to note that subaltern Christological insights based on the life and ministry of Jesus of Nazareth hold the promise of creating a better path for the liberation of subalterns in Asia.

Postcolonial Christology

In the Western world, Richard Horsley, Sharon Ringe, Fernando F. Segovia, Stephen D. Moore and Elisabeth Schüssler Fiorenza are among those who have made significant contributions in the field of postcolonial Christology. Horsley's readings of Mark and Paul from a postcolonial point of view have challenged many. Segovia and Mary Ann Tolbert have edited three substantial volumes of essays contributed by leading practitioners of biblical hermeneutics from both the West and the postcolonial world, respectively titled *Reading from this Place*, Volumes I and II (1995), and *Teaching the Bible* (1998). These volumes presented many challenges, arising from issues such as reading the Bible from the margins, the role of the reader in biblical interpretation, the developing of new methodologies, and ideologies for tracing insights from the Bible in order to bring about the liberation of the oppressed. Most of the major strands of Asian Christology, such as those described above, come under the category of postcolonial Christology, as postcolonial Christology addresses the issue of the boundaries between various groups of people.

Conclusion

The birds'-eye view of Asian Christologies presented in the foregoing pages has shown the fascinating operation of historical imagination by Asians on the person and work of Jesus Christ, rooted in their ongoing life struggles in the Asian context/s. What has emerged is that issues relating to gender, class, caste, race, plurality of cultures and religions have played a significant role in enabling biblical readers in Asia to arrive at inspiring and contextually relevant images of Jesus of Nazareth, images which relate to the diverse Asian contexts and accompany the oppressed in their struggles for life and dignity.

❓ SUGGESTED QUESTIONS

1 What are the various factors that have led to the development of contextual Christologies in Asia?

2 What are the major features of liberation Christologies?

3 Asian women have recovered the feminine aspects of Christ and have thus, according to Kwok Pui-lan, 'destabilized the gender of Christ'. What, in your view, are the problems and the promises of such Christological constructions?

4 Define the term subaltern. Subaltern Christologies in Asia have focused on images of the vulnerable and suffering Christ in the context of their own peoples' struggles. Do you have any such examples in your own context? How have the marginalized in your own context understood Christ as their liberator?

5 How have people in your own context used cultural resources to construct contextual images of Jesus Christ?

Part 3
New seeds in the furrows

9
Between a rock and a hard place: an Asian theology of survival

Gemma Tulud Cruz

 Abstract

Cruz draws attention in her essay to the Asian paradox of widespread poverty amid the growing economic prosperity created by the forces of globalization. Identifying the Asian experience from a theological perspective as a *via crucis* (way of the cross) marked by suffering, she explores how people on the margins disproportionately bear the burden of Asia's poverty and focuses on the various strategies of survival adopted by those who suffer. Paying particular attention to the various strategies of survival – such as silence, humour and laughter, stories, songs and dance – which have been adopted by women at the margins, she goes on to discuss Asian theology as a 'theology of survival' or a 'theology of survival quality of life'.

 Via crucis: the Asian context

At first glance Asia presents a fascinating picture. Encompassing one-third of the land area of the globe, it is the world's largest and, not surprisingly, most populous continent. It is home to almost 60 per cent of humanity, many of whom live in about twenty megacities, which have populations of around 5 to 20 million. Asia is equally impressive in its cultural and religious diversity. It has seven major linguistic zones and an array of dialects or local languages. It is also the birthplace of and a continuing haven for the world's major religions.

Economically things seem to be rosy for Asia as well. With the second largest economy in the world (Japan), more than one tiger economy (for example Singapore and South Korea), and rising economic superpowers (China and India), global analysts even predict that the twenty-first century will be the Asian century. Yet within and beneath all this seeming prosperity is abject poverty and misery. As the Asian Conference of Third World

75

Theologians asserts in 'Asia's Struggle for Full Humanity: Toward a Relevant Theology':

> Asia suffers under the heels of forced poverty. Its life has been truncated by centuries of colonialism and a more recent neocolonialism. Its cultures are marginalized, its social relations distorted. The cities with their miserable slums, swollen with poor peasants driven off the land, constitute a picture of wanton affluence side by side with abject poverty that is common to the majority of Asia's countries. (Asian Conference of Third World Theologians, 1980: 101)

The 2006 report on the UN Millennium Development Goals in Asia gives a more concrete and contemporary face to this lamentable situation. According to the report 620 million Asians, two-thirds of the world's poor, live on less than $1 a day, while the continent has a huge share of the global population living in rural areas with poor sanitation, underweight children and malnourished adults. India alone, the report goes on to say, is home to 38 per cent of the world's total of underweight children under the age of five, and has more than double the number of illiterate women (15–24 years old) than any other subregion of the world. Moreover, Asia accounts for more than two-thirds of the world's TB cases and deaths (SOLC, 2010).

Today this unequal distribution of wealth is made sharper by globalization as many Asian nations become dependent on foreign investment and groan under the weight of increasing indebtedness to the World Bank and the International Monetary Fund. The crushing poverty caused by corrupt governments, unemployment and rising prices is then exploited by multinational corporations, who outsource and build sprawling free trade zones that are beyond the reach of labour laws, thereby intensifying Asian people's exploitation.

Politically, there continue to be varying degrees of freedom and unfreedom across the Asian continent. This is due mainly to the kaleidoscope of forms of government that make up Asia's political landscape; these range from democracies to theocratic, monarchical and communist regimes, and to military juntas. Without a doubt, however, widespread militarization and authoritarianism accounts for many tragic aspects of the Asian context, for example political persecution, abduction, torture, killings, massacres and genocide.

> In fact from Pakistan to Korea, passing through the subcontinent and Southeast Asia, practically all parliamentary governments, with the exception of Japan, have at some time given way to military governments or authoritarian regimes of one form or the other. In these countries not only are political rights suppressed, but so also are the rights of workers to strike in the cities and the rights of peasants to organize themselves in the countryside. Many leaders and people holding political views contrary to the ruling group are condemned to spend several years in prison, without due process or trial.
> (Asian Conference of Third World Theologians, 1980: 102)

In many cases weapons that kill their very own people eat up Asian countries' national budgets, as has been seen in the bloody repression of demonstrators in China in Tiananmen Square in 1989, in Myanmar in 2007 and in Thailand in 2010.

> What is clear is that the Asian context, from a theological perspective, is a via crucis (way of the cross), for it is undeniably marked by suffering. It cannot be denied that this pervasive suffering, which Sri Lankan theologian Aloysius Pieris aptly calls the 'Calvary of Asian poverty', falls disproportionately on a number of groups that have been progressively pushed into the margins, particularly women, unskilled migrant (especially undocumented) workers, refugees and indigenous peoples.

Nat Yogachandra, for instance, points out that despite some progress made by women's movements, nearly two-thirds of adult Asian women are illiterate and the percentage of girls enrolled in Asia's primary schools is far below that in every other region of the world except sub-Saharan Africa (Yogachandra, 2003). As Filipina feminist theologian Mary John Mananzan argues, although the situation may vary from country to country 'it is safe to say that in the home, society, and the church, [Asian] women are still second class citizens' (Mananzan, 1998: 13, 14).

In the case of tribal/indigenous peoples, Indian theologian Wati Longchar contends that these are the most exploited people in the world, because they have suffered discrimination, genocide, exploitation and alienation at various stages of their history. I have noted in my book *An Intercultural Theology of Migration: Pilgrims in the Wilderness* (2010) that many Asian migrant workers (especially those that are unskilled and remain unaccounted for in official figures), in the meantime, not only provide contemporary globalization with circulating and expendable capital, but are also their countries' primary exports, thereby earning them the label 'disposable people'. Consequently for these groups life is often not merely a matter of struggle but also a question of survival. In the next section I shall attempt to make sense of the different ways in which these groups forge a survival quality of life, looking especially at that life as experienced by women.

Living in the midst of dying: surviving in the margins

So how do people on the margins survive? In other words, how do they create some semblance of a quality of life in the face of systematic oppression? I will try to answer these questions by examining the ways in which certain marginalized groups in Asia refuse to give in completely to their oppression. More specifically, I will discuss some of the subtle but powerful strategies with which these groups resist, particularly those that at first glance may look negative or weak but are actually potent.

Yale professor and anthropologist James Scott calls these strategies 'hidden transcripts'. By this term he refers to a politics of disguise and anonymity among subordinate groups that is partly sanitized, ambiguous and coded. He says this is often expressed in rumours, gossip, folktales, jokes, songs, rituals, codes and euphemisms that usually come from folk culture. These, according to Scott, contain not only speech acts but also a whole range of practices that contravene the public transcript (the regular, everyday encounters and interactions between individuals) of the dominant society (Scott, 1990: 19).

The aforementioned marginalized groups employ a number of these strategies. The first is silence. Consider the following examples given by Mary John Mananzan, wherein silence is utilized by Asian women as part of their mobilization and campaigning against the destructive mechanisms and effects of globalization. Indian women of the Chipko movement embraced the trees of the Himalayas to save them from being cut down by logging companies. In the Philippines, meanwhile, the indigenous women of the Cordillera took now legendary protest action against the building of the Chico River Dam: when the protesting women were confronted by the military, they took off their blouses at a signal from their leader, startling the men and causing them to run away (Mananzan, 1998a: 121).

Upon closer scrutiny these protests prove to have been clothed in silence. There was no need for words and this very absence of words, I believe, made the protests all the more dramatic and eloquent. Even the Asian women theologians of the Ecumenical Association of Third World Theologians (EATWOT) employed this kind of strategy when, as part of their resistance to the marginalization of women's experience and perspective within the organization, they walked out in silence during the association's 1996 general assembly (Mananzan, 1998b: 18).

Humour and laughter, particularly as expressed through jokes, is another hidden strategy employed by marginalized groups in Asia when dealing with their oppression. In a presentation on women and globalization, for example, an American student of mine showed video footage of a centre in Nepal which helps Nepalese women victims of trafficking and prostitution in India who are unable or ashamed to return to their families. What struck me in the video was how the women were laughing and making fun of themselves in the midst of their tragic situation. Filipina domestic workers in Hong Kong, who are not alien to unjust, sometimes slave-like conditions, create jokes to mitigate their oppression by manipulating the language. They jokingly substitute, for example, the Tagalog word *unggoy*, which means 'monkey', for the Cantonese *m'goi*, which can be translated as 'please', 'thank you' or 'excuse me', in various situations where they are usually victimized or discriminated against by the local Chinese. These places include restaurants, where they may summon the Chinese waiter by saying '*Unggoy, unggoy!*' The waiter will probably understand this as a polite but poorly pronounced attempt to get his attention by saying 'Excuse me' or 'Please.' Having made the waiter respond to the epithet 'monkey', the domestic helpers feel that they have outsmarted him, and hence break into smiles or burst into laughter (Constable, 1997: 176).

Last but not least, stories, songs and dance are employed by marginalized Asians to help them survive their oppression. Gabriele Dietrich gives an example of the use of song and dance in India, where she shares her riveting experience of witnessing young and old women who, amid pouring rain, danced to songs and slogans during the 17-year struggle of the Adivasi people against the building of the Sardar Sarovar Dam (Dietrich, 2003). Stories, in the meantime, are vital to Korean women's survival strategies. Not surprisingly, and as Moon Hee-Suk maintains, the Korean liberationist theology known as Minjung theology, which focuses on the experiences of the Minjung, 'begins by listening to the *minjung*'s stories, which tell of the sad and desperate situation of the poor' (Moon, 2010).

> In the face of pervasive and multi-dimensional forms of oppression, what could be construed as the resistance strategies of marginalized Asian groups are clearly often employed in the name of survival.

To speak of survival is to talk about 'limit' situations or about living on the 'boundary', the 'verge' or the 'brink', where in many cases it is a matter of life and death or a question of living in the midst of dying. Life and dignity for groups living in such situations, in other words, is about preserving the life and integrity of self, family and community, so much so that survival becomes the highest ethical value.

> The theology or God-talk that arises from marginalized groups in Asia could then be also regarded as a theology of survival or a theology of survival quality of life.

In the next section I shall elaborate on this aspect of Asian theology.

 ## Life on the edge as God-talk: Asian theology as a theology of survival

In her critically acclaimed book *Sisters in the Wilderness*, African-American theologian Delores Williams speaks of the theology of survival quality of life, a theology that is constituted in the attempts of oppressed people, families and/or communities to arrive at well-being through the use of, search for and/or creation of supportive spiritual, economic, political, legal or educational resources. These attempts or survival strategies, Williams says, employ an art of cunning (with the use of skill and imagination), an art of encounter (involving resistance and endurance), an art of care (manifested in commitment and charity) and an art of connecting (through connecting the oppressed) (Williams, 1993: 236, 237).

As such, and as could be seen in the examples of 'hidden transcripts' in the preceding section, an Asian theology of survival is about courage and creativity. In the first place a survival quality of life is about 'making a way out of no way'. Moreover, an Asian theology of survival is about faith and community, as it is a way of individually and collectively dealing with oppressive conditions whereby religion is used to make sense of and survive the oppression and life events are infused with religious meanings. Most importantly, in an Asian theology of survival God's support is sought to the point that God becomes the element of necessity and trust in God is complete. As Williams herself asserts, survival struggle and/or struggle for quality of life are inseparable and are associated with God's presence with the community. The Bible and the Christian tradition sheds light on this survivalist God-talk through the many stories of individuals and communities who struggled for survival in courageously creative ways, from Hagar and the Israelites who fought for physical survival, to the early Christian communities throughout the Roman Empire who had to struggle for physical and religious survival in the face of religious persecution.

The story and person of Hagar are especially used by Williams to drive home the point of the religious nature of the survival quality of life. According to Williams, Hagar shows that the capacity to envision resources for survival in the midst of scarcity involves more than the human will alone (Gen. 21.18–19), also requiring revelation from a God that provides insight and vision into one's socio-historical and geographical situation. Williams goes on to say that while there is potential for despair, the gift of vision allows for renewed hope in the midst of wilderness experiences (Williams, 1993: 28–32).

Aside from Scripture and tradition, culture also obviously plays an important role in an Asian theology of survival. The survival strategies laid out in the preceding section, for example, are heavily rooted in the context of particular groups and places. And as Wati Longchar insists, particularly in the case of tribal/indigenous peoples, 'the experience of oppression and hardships, stories, myths, symbols, dances, songs, and the tribal/indigenous people's spirituality have become vital sources for doing theology' (Longchar, 2002: 6).

In talking about the struggle for survival of Hispanic women as a critical lens for a Hispanic women's liberation theology, Cuban-American theologian Ada Maria Isasi-Diaz even argues for a hermeneutic of survival in evaluating culture from within (Isasi-Diaz, 1993: 16–22). Having said this, an Asian theology of survival then requires the recognition of culture as a site of struggle. In the face of the legacies of both colonialism and neocolonialism, an Asian theology of survival demands the recovery and mediation of cultural practices that continue to be subjected to 'institutional forgetting', especially those that are devalued by or contradict the dominant consciousness.

Silence is an example of this. It can be the antithesis of words or aggression, which are usually the normal and accepted (but very Western) modes of resistance. Even if it is presented as a form of passive resistance, for example as cold obedience on the surface and seething defiance underneath, silence will probably not garner positive consideration in Western feminist theological circles, where passivity is not highly valued. Without a doubt silence is problematic when framed within the discourse on violence against women. But when all the ways in which silence is engaged by Asians are taken into account, one might see that it can be seen as a form of resistance or, at the very least, a component of active resistance.

Nantawan Boonprasat Lewis in her article 'On Naming Justice: The Spiritual and Political Connection in Violence against Asian Immigrant Women', for instance, even describes silence as a new meaning to Asian resistance and liberation. Lewis contends that certain Asian cultural expressions, such as silence, have been understood as indications of submissiveness, subservience and obedience, and that this has been questioned by feminist scholars as a misreading of the 'hidden transcripts' that some women have used as resources for survival (Lewis, 2003: 485).

> An Asian theology of survival, in other words, is imaginative and entails a hermeneutics of rupture. It resists the perennial danger of domesticating negativity or disingenuously dismissing seemingly innocuous cultural practices.

Truly, silence speaks, humour and laughter destabilize, while songs, stories and dance narrate, mourn and celebrate life's triumphs and tragedies. They are ways of questioning, finding and insisting on the sacred in our life experiences. Such an approach to God-talk on the margins rightly gives a much deserved honour and place, I believe, to the 'theologically oppressed' – the everyday theologians – the people in the trenches who are struggling not just to live real lives but to literally survive amid the incongruities and injustices of our time.

SUGGESTED QUESTIONS

1 What is the impact of poverty in the Asian context?

2 Do you agree with the author that the Asian context from the perspective of theology is a *via crucis* (way of the cross)? Why?

3 What are the strategies used by those on the margins to survive and create a semblance of a quality of life in the face of systemic evil?

4 Reflect upon what the author means by 'life on the edge as God-talk' and discern its relevance to your own context.

5 Can you think of how silence, jokes and dance can be alternative sources of resistance and survival for the oppressed communities in your own context?

10
Indigenous theology in Asia: issues and perspectives

Wati Longchar

 Abstract

Longchar defines indigenous people as 'first people' or original settlers and, using concrete examples, provides an overview of the various challenges that they face in the context of globalization. After identifying the various stages in the development of indigenous peoples' theologies, namely the receiving stage (1800s–1950s), the learning stage (1950s–1980s) and the self-theologizing stage (post 1980s), he moves on to describe the kinds of theology that indigenous peoples need. He brings out the distinctive features of indigenous peoples' theologies, most importantly the perspective of land, which shapes their views of liberation and identity, along with the creation-centred and people-centred theological perspectives they exemplify.

 Who are we?

It is good to start by asking, who are we? How are we defined by others? How do we define ourselves? Indigenous peoples constitute about 5 to 8 per cent of the world population. The identity of indigenous people is a matter that often causes confusion. There is no universally accepted definition of 'indigenous people'. They are variously identified as tribals, ethnic minorities, native, aborigines or 'Indians', names given by colonizers, Western missionaries and anthropologists. Sometimes indigenous people are also identified as cultural minorities, hill tribes, mountain peoples, forest/remote area dwellers, and so forth. All these identities are given by the dominant society, and especially by people who live in urban or semi-urban contexts. Such categories are however rarely accepted by the people concerned as generic terms applicable to themselves. Indigenous people identify themselves by their own names, for example Hakka, Amis, Thao, Aos, Chin, Laos, Mizos, Khasis or Ainus.

> When we speak of 'indigenous people' we mean the first people or the original settlers of any particular land, those who gave names to their mountains, rivers, rocks and trees. The naming of a child is the right of the parents. Naming is always connected to ownership, caring and parenting. Each name is associated with an event and identity. Those name givers are called indigenous people.

✳ Context: indigenous peoples in today's world

Let me begin this section with a story. A group of indigenous theologians assembled for a conference to be held from 21 to 26 October 2008 at Baguio in the Philippines. When we arrived in the city of Baguio, we were informed that one of our indigenous brothers, James Balao, had been abducted because he spoke for justice. Balao was an active researcher and trainer of the Cordillera People's Alliance (CPA), and his research fed into the organization's campaigns to expose the wrongdoing of multinational companies and the government and to assert the land and resources rights of the indigenous people. It should be noted that indigenous peoples are often left landless and deprived of their means of livelihood because of the widespread destruction of the forests by multinational companies in the name of development projects.

This is not an isolated incident. The global history of human rights abuse against indigenous peoples and their activities has always revealed an element of corporate and government collusion. Whether in Australia, Taiwan, India or the USA, all indigenous peoples have had similar experiences. Their ancestors have suffered discrimination, genocide, exploitation and alienation at various stages of their history. The suffering of indigenous people began in some countries even before the European invasion; for example, in India the history of defeat of Dalits and Adivasis (Tribals) began at the hands of Aryan invaders almost 3,500 years ago. In the course of history, the indigenous people became hewers of wood and drawers of water, and the nomads became kings and princes, masters and aristocrats. Today they are further marginalized through the processes of the global capital regime.

The global empire and the greed of global capital are having a tremendous impact on the geopolitics of the world, and are destroying and threatening all life, especially that of the poor and marginalized such as indigenous communities. In today's world, 'growth' is considered to be the only principle for liberation. The concepts of 'care for one another', 'just economy' and '(sabbath) rest for creation' are considered to be non-productive and are regarded as the root of all human problems, from poverty to sickness and political instability. The global market turns not only the earth's resources but indigenous peoples and our cultural activities into commodities for profit. Let me next cite some examples of the barbaric atrocities, violations of human rights, ethnic conflicts, poverty, injustice, low self-esteem, feelings of inferiority, and alienation from an earth-centred life and spirituality that are the interconnected results of globalization.

Denial of religious rights

Though indigenous people's religion is the oldest religion in existence and has a distinct spirituality, it is still considered as the lowest form of religion and is often not given due recognition as 'religion'. In the city of Medan, Indonesia, an indigenous community known as the Parmalin are struggling to construct a place of worship. They are denied the right to worship on the grounds that their religion is not registered under the government and their traditional places of worship are the forests, not cities or towns; so they are told they should go back to the forest. Interestingly, the people opposing the work are mainly Christians. The construction of a place of worship remains half done.

Again, there is a minority religion called Sundan that belongs to the indigenous Sundanese people. Because the government does not recognize their religion, they are unable to get official marriage certificates and their children are seen as illegitimate. Indigenous religions are still considered as 'animist', which is why in many countries they cannot be registered under the government as religions. This is an offence to indigenous people and an act of ignorance.

In some countries, like India, indigenous people are being denied the right of propagating and professing their faith. Majority groups can participate in re-conversion, but these minorities cannot. In India, indigenous religions are still considered as an offshoot of Hinduism, though tribal people have a distinct culture and religion. Conversion to Christianity is seen as a threat justifying re-conversion to Hinduism, including forced conversion.

Disappearance of language

A major function of language is to act as a reservoir for people's identity and self-expression. It helps people to dream their own dreams and assists them to articulate their hopes and visions of a new future. Language is also one of the most important social agencies that create feelings of community by providing identity (Joseph, n.d.: 6). Indigenous peoples' languages are fast disappearing. Today a native American language known as Euchee is spoken only by five individuals. In the name of national integration, the military junta in Myanmar does not allow children to be taught in their ethnic languages.

Some indigenous communities have intentionally adopted the language of the dominant community out of fear of discrimination. The adoption by Taiwanese people of four or five personal names corresponding to the country's different colonial masters is a good example. The confiscation in Taiwan of vernacular Bibles and the prohibition of the printing of the Bible in local languages (as a contravention of the policy to promote the use of the national language) testifies to the way in which the dominant society attempts to destroy people's right to their own language.

The use of local languages has not only been forcefully denied, but people have also been led to believe that the use and command of a local language exposes their inferior position in society. Can we expect indigenous peoples' cultures and value systems to survive without a language? With the loss of language, indigenous peoples lose their distinct social, cultural and spiritual values.

Denial of ancestral land

Most indigenous people have lost their land due to abuse of the legal system, development activities and political manipulation. The land struggle of the Aboriginal people in Australia has a long history. The ongoing conflict in Mindanao in the Philippines focuses on the struggle of the Bangsamoro people for self-determination and entitlement to their ancestral lands. Today several indigenous peoples are being forcefully evicted from their lands. Sometimes fear and tension are created to drive them away. With the loss of the land which is the main source of their livelihood and culture, indigenous people today constitute the world's biggest labour force; they work illegally or unaccounted for as migrant workers in many countries and constitute the poorest sections of society.

Denial of identity

The Japanese government has declared that there is only one homogenous community in Japan, denying the existence of peoples like the Ainu and other indigenous communities. Japan is yet to recognize that the Ainu 'are an indigenous people with a distinct language, religion and culture' (Fogarty, 2008). In the name of national integration, the existence of the first settlers in Taiwan and Nepal is being ignored and denied. As a result, ten or more tribes in Taiwan who have been living in the island for two to three thousand years, and more than 100 tribes in Nepal with distinct cultures and traditions, are being denied their identity. More than 500 Adivasi and Dalit communities in India are categorized as Hindus. Likewise, most indigenous people have been assimilated into their dominant society in the name of national integration – under the Chinese culture in Taiwan, the Hindu caste system in India, the Burmese culture in Myanmar, Hinduism in Nepal, and the Islamic culture in Bangladesh, Indonesia, Malaysia, etc.

Many indigenous people are afraid to disclose their identity. After a friend of mine wrote an excellent article on indigenous peoples' struggle in Myanmar, I sought permission for its publication in the *Journal of Tribal Studies*. He wrote back to me saying, 'You are permitted to publish but change my name to an Indian name. Otherwise, I will be arrested.' People who once had a rich cultural tradition are now reduced to 'no-people' in many countries.

The sex trade

In Thailand, Cambodia, Myanmar, Nepal and India, it is estimated that more than 40 per cent of indigenous girls and women who migrate to the cities in search of a better living, end up working in the sex trade. The majority of women trafficked across state borders in Asia are from indigenous communities. Having been reduced to abject poverty, many of them have no option except to sell their bodies. Today many have become victims of HIV & AIDS.

> When discussing indigenous people we are talking about people who are being crushed and who are denied their land, culture, language and identity. We cannot do indigenous theology without addressing such individual and collective oppression, denial and abuse of power.

Do we address those issues in our theologizing? The history of Christianity among indigenous peoples is between 150 and 250 years old. Christian missionaries were the first to come and work for the liberation of the people. They transformed indigenous societies by abolishing evil practices such as slavery, headhunting and excessive feasting. Many modern institutions were first introduced by the Church – the first school, the first hospital, the first translation work and the first printing press among many others. These all changed traditional societies.

> However, Christian missions, no matter which denomination or society they belonged to, considered themselves 'superior' and consistently maintained an exclusive attitude towards indigenous religion and culture.

They came determined to conquer the 'other world' by Christian faith. Conversion was understood in terms of replacement of the old ways of life, including the rejection of traditional cultures and value systems. Today, as a result, many people have forgotten and been uprooted from their traditional value systems.

Indigenous peoples' theology and its development

Indigenous theology is a newcomer to the theological scene and theology emerging among these alienated minorities may be called 'indigenous peoples' theology'. Born out of indigenous peoples' experiences of various forms of injustice and exploitation in the context of their assertion for right and identity, it is a theology that attempts to express the Christian faith in indigenous socio-cultural, religious, traditional and liturgical thought patterns. Indigenous peoples' theology is a liberation and resistance theology – resistance to affirm justice, identity, dignity and the wholeness of the land and all its inhabitants. Indigenous peoples' experiences of oppression and hardship, traditional stories, myths, symbols, dances and songs, and their connectedness to the land and environment, become vital resources for doing theology. Such theology reflects on the issue of these peoples' ethnic, cultural and political identities. The people, the land and the sacred power to give them hope are the main elements in these theologies.

We may divide the history of the development of Christian theology among indigenous people roughly into three stages.

The receiving stage (1800–1950s)

During this period, the churches were under the control of Western missionaries. In their effort to contextualize theology, missionaries pursued the 'Translation Method' of doing theology. Perceiving Western culture as superior and as the only valid expression of the Christian faith, they attempted to translate the theological formulations of their 'mother' churches abroad in appropriate native languages by adopting and adapting local terminologies, idioms and categories (Jathanna, 1986: 71).

It was thought that the Christian faith as developed in the West was *the unchanging truth for all ages and all contexts*, and should be accepted without question. Therefore, native cultures and traditions were never considered valuable resources for doing theology. Christians who participated in traditional festivals were excommunicated from the Church. Drums, traditional songs, dances and value systems were condemned as evils and prohibited among believers. There was very little or no awareness of the religio-cultural experience of the people. Theology was alien to the people; it spoke an alien language and expressed alien ideas. Theology was outside the people's reality. God's revelation was accepted in a very narrow way, reducing indigenous peoples' religion and culture to mere *preparatio evangelii*.

The learning stage (1950s–1980s)

During the 1950s and 1960s, with the growth of various national movements and efforts towards post-independence reconstruction, the struggle for self-identity and the indigenization or enculturation of theology became a priority for the churches. During this period, as many Western missionaries left their mission work, more space was created for local people to exercise their rights, responsibilities and leadership in the Church. In this period the native church experimented with different models of theology.

The *philosophical model* was born in the wake of nationalism, in which many theologians in the Global South became critical of missionary theology and began in doing theology to import philosophical concepts, doctrines and symbols from other religions, especially Hinduism and Buddhism.

Unfortunately, like the dominant theological reflections in the West, such theological approaches became abstract intellectual exercises unrelated to the real-life situation of the people. Indigenous peoples' view of life and spirituality were undermined, not being considered philosophically deep enough to articulate theology, and were discarded in the process of doing contextual theology. People studied indigenous culture and beliefs simply from the traditional missiological perspective, as a dark world to be conquered, and could not imagine that the cultural values and spirituality of indigenous people could help in contextualizing the Christian faith in their cultural setting. Such a one-sided theological paradigm alienated indigenous people from their own religions and cultures.

In the 1970s and 1980s the advocates of interfaith theology made a significant contribution, employing the *dialogical model* of doing theology. A central theological claim of this model is that unless it takes into account the unacknowledged riches of God's work with the whole of humanity and other aspects of God's creation, Christian theology cannot become authentic and liberative. Although advocates of the dialogical method were not always sympathetic and sensitive to indigenous peoples' spirituality, culture and religion, its affirmation of God's revelation and lordship over the world and in all cultures and religions widened understanding of the mystery of God. This understanding enabled its practitioners to appreciate and respect the differences of others and also their own spirituality, religion and culture.

The self-theologizing stage (post 1980s)

After the departure of the missionaries (which took place during the missionary era itself in some churches), many churches launched the three-self movement (self-government, self-supporting and self-propagation). Many churches were thereby enabled to stand on their own feet in terms of support and mission. However, one important element which was left out of this movement was 'self-theologizing', which until recently was not considered an important component of a church's self-identity. It was only in the 1980s, under the influence of liberation theology, that churches recognized the importance of 'self-theologizing' in rooting the Church and its mission in the actual life of the people.

Initially, liberation theology in Asia was greatly influenced and shaped by Latin American methodology. However, indigenous communities, women and other marginalized movements have widened the horizon of liberation theology from its Latin American origins. Along with economic and political issues, the cultural and religious dimensions of discrimination are taken seriously in liberation theologies. They have influenced people to reread Scripture from the perspective of the poor and oppressed in their struggle for justice and freedom. Commitment to victims, to the oppressed and struggling poor, as the basis and starting point of theology has inspired alienated indigenous peoples to discover their identity, their rights and their dignity. It has motivated people to engage themselves in new ways of doing theology by relating the gospel to social, political and cultural realities. However, this theological paradigm is very limited and is not capable of addressing all the issues of indigenous people. Therefore, we need to explore new ways of doing indigenous theology.

What kind of theology do we need?

We need a people-centred theology, a theology centred on the vision of our Lord Jesus Christ. Theological concepts developed within the dominant theological discourses legitimized a religion for the benefit of the masters and rulers, and sanctioned the exploitation and manipulation of all aspects of God's creation for the extraction of maximum profit. We may cite three examples of this:

The concept of God: Theology is God-talk, a discourse on God. The dominant images of God developed in Christian traditions are images such as Ruler, Lord, Master and Warrior. They are all patriarchal, political, military images. These images have made Christianity a religion of and for the ruler, the elite and the upper class. Such rulers' theologies have supported colonial governments, war, invasion and the unprecedented exploitation of the earth's resources. Such imperial constructs of the concept of God will not be capable of liberating either the people or nature from unjust systems and exploitative practices.

The understanding of mission: Discourse on God as ruler and master has reinforced a success-oriented or triumphalistic mission. Terms like 'Mission Crusade', 'Mission Campaign', 'Home Penetration', 'Mass Evangelization' are military language and concepts which have caused mission to be regarded as a conquest of other religions and cultures. Mission has been exclusive and has failed to recognize God's revelation in other religious traditions and cultures. Mission is God's mission. But Christians have acted as if we are the owners of mission.

The understanding of creation: The dominant Christian interpretation of creation is anthropocentric or human-centred. Thus it is held that nature exists for the benefit of humans, and that apart from rational beings, the other elements of God's creation cannot come under the scheme of salvation. There is no sacredness and mystery in nature, which can therefore be manipulated and controlled for the benefit of human beings; indeed, to exploit nature is an expression of divine will. This one-sided theological interpretation again justifies the expansion of colonial power and the exploitation of nature. The ideology of globalization and the expansion of global capital markets are deeply rooted in this interpretation.

Discourse on indigenous theology can make a difference today by turning and rerouting theology to the Jesus of Galilee movement. In Jesus' movement, we see a decisive reversal of focus from the empire and money to people in pain, from ruler to ruled, from oppressor to oppressed, from individualism to a cosmic vision of life. Jesus' movement was a people-centred and cosmic-centred movement against the power of destruction and death.

> We must reroute indigenous theologies towards the ethics of the Jesus movement in the context of people in pain and the groaning of God's creation. The option for 'people in pain' and the 'groaning creation' as the locus of indigenous theology requires sacrifice and a radical departure from power, institutionalism and Mammon.

The distinctive identity of indigenous peoples' theology

As indigenous peoples' theology is a contextual theology, a theology from 'below' and from the 'underside of history', it aims to liberate indigenous peoples from their inferiority complex, from oppression and discrimination, by attempting to rediscover the liberative motifs in their cultures and religion, and by reinterpreting the Bible and Christian traditions from the perspective of the people. And in the process of working for their own liberation and transformation, and for their creative participation in wider society, indigenous people work for the liberation of both the oppressors and the oppressed. It is, therefore, a theology that includes the liberation of all humanity and of God's entire creation.

> Methodologically speaking, the point of departure of indigenous theology, in contrast to other contextual theologies, is that indigenous theology seeks liberation from the perspective of 'land' because it is the land that sustains and nourishes people and gives them an identity.

Among indigenous peoples, their history, culture, religion and spirituality, even their sacred power, cannot be conceived without 'creation/land' or 'space'. The land and its inhabitants are two aspects of one reality. Human liberation will be void and empty unless it affirms the integrity of the goodness of the land and its resources. Liberation without land is not liberation. It will lead to slavery and destruction. Therefore, the land and its resources, which sustain and nourish all beings and give them an identity and selfhood, is not merely a justice issue to be set alongside other similar concerns. It is the foundation of history, existence and identity (Tinker, 1981 and 1994).

Poverty, war, oppression, ethnic conflict and identity problems cannot be understood or solved without relating them to the integrity of creation/land. Justice to creation/land becomes central to liberation and human dignity, and to the fullness of life (Eidger, 2007). That is why doing justice to 'land' is the starting point of indigenous peoples' theology and their search for liberation. It is essential to give methodological priority to achieving justice with respect to land not only because of such peoples' 'earth-centred' world-view and tradition, but because of the contemporary ecological crisis, the misuse of resources, the current market culture, the war for oil and the survival crisis facing many people. This methodological priority of doing justice to the totality of creation is the primary departure of indigenous peoples' theology from other contextual theologies.

❋ The absence of spiritual connection with earth's family

A crucial element missing from Christian theologies today is the spiritual connection with the mystery of the earth's family. The students of the School of Peace in Bangalore, an interfaith peace school conducted by the Asia Pacific Alliance of YMCAs and the Interfaith Cooperation Forum, wanted to plan a programme for International Earth Day. The students came up with many suggestions, some of which were:

- an appeal to all people, including those in high positions, to use bicycles for a day;
- organizing street drama on environmental issues;
- organizing programmes whereby each person would plant a tree;
- painting themes related to environmental protection on T-shirts;
- organizing essay competitions on environmental protection;
- art competitions for children;
- encouraging people to write and publish articles, poems and stories related to environmental protection;
- organizing concerts and public lectures to raise awareness;
- encouraging people to take public buses instead of using private cars;
- creating an awareness campaign about the danger of plastic bags, etc.;
- organizing a week-long environmental awareness bicycle tour for young people;
- eating only vegetables.

Though these are excellent ideas, what is missing from them is any spiritual connection with the earth. I therefore started thinking about how indigenous people observed Earth Day in the past. All the activities were deeply religious. Some indigenous communities used to celebrate Earth Day for

between three and six days. The earth was given complete rest and treated with respect by observing the following instructions:
- no one was allowed to cut firewood lest the earth be shaken;
- the use of axes and knives was prohibited;
- no one was allowed to penetrate the earth using a spear or any pointed instrument;
- no one was allowed to make noise;
- no one was allowed to spit on the ground;
- no one was allowed to stamp on the ground harshly;
- no one was allowed to make fire on the ground;
- no one was to have sex;
- no killing of animals was permitted;
- no trees were to be cut down;
- no one was allowed to work in the fields;
- no merrymaking – dancing, singing, etc. – was to take place.

The earth was to be honoured and treated as sacred. It was on these days that peace and reconciliation initiatives took place between individuals, clans, villages and communities. Earth Day was also a day of prayer and contemplation. This was and still is part of the culture of tribal people. Rejection of this spiritual connection with the earth's family in development activities will be a serious setback for the future survival of the world.

Unless we as individuals rediscover our spiritual connection with the earth's family, it is not possible to talk about liberation and a community where all people are treated justly. It is like attempting to liberate oneself after killing one's mother. This means from indigenous peoples' perspective that an authentic Christian theology is possible only in relation to protection of the land.

Our theological perspective

No one person or community can have a monopoly over theology. To express knowledge of God in one's own way is the inherent right of all human beings. We can comprehend God on the basis both of what God did to our ancestors even before the arrival of Christianity and what God is doing for the people in our concrete historical context. Therefore, we are called to articulate our faith journey with God and community in our own way.

The biblical testimony of creation

Indigenous communities recognize several 'scriptures', including oral traditions, in their efforts to comprehend God. The Bible is the book of indigenous people. It speaks of people's relationship in society, cultivation, animals, nature and encounter with the divine power in their search for liberation. The Hebrew

Bible starts with the creation of heaven and earth, and moves on to an account of the creation of humanity from the ground/land, asserting that humanity is created in God's image and that each race and nation has been assigned a space in God's world (Deut. 32.8). The land, from whose womb humanity was formed (Gen. 2.7), is viewed in the Bible as truly alive. It is not a mass of dead matter, but a living, pulsating organism. Through our land-centred lenses, the mountains and hills and trees can be seen to sing and clap their hands. These are not mere metaphors or poetry. The land, the whole creation, is alive, and is so intimately woven with the lives and struggles of indigenous communities that it groans in travail (Romans 8.19, 22) whenever we, the people of the land, suffer displacement, alienation, exploitation, exile and persecution.

The New Testament gospel, too, proclaims how central the redemption of the margins is in the divine economy. Jesus always located his ministry within the context and world-view of farming or fishing. Jesus' language, metaphors and symbols are drawn from the day-to-day experiences of farmers and fisher-folk and their struggle for justice against the empire. In other words, the Judaeo-Christian gospel of the reign of God is affirmative of our indigenous world-view and of the spirituality that constructs our understanding of who we are and what we struggle for.

God in creation

Creation is the first act of God's revelation. God cannot be perceived without water, wind, trees, vegetation, sky, light, darkness, animals or humans. In this first act of revelation, God revealed himself/herself as *co-creator* with the earth. The most striking aspect in this first act of God's revelation is that 'God is present in creation'. The presence of God makes the earth sacred. That is why God entered into covenant relationship with all creatures. There are many stories, myths, parables, even fairy tales, that relate how the 'Sacred Power' and the land sustain life together. This is what makes us join with Isaiah and say 'the whole earth is full of his glory' (Isa. 6.3). Indigenous people always conceive of God-world in a manner which is very closely related their everyday lives. Totems, taboos and other customary laws once tied them together as one whole. To perceive God as detached from creation/earth or to understand God as a mere transcendental being who controls life from above is no part of the biblical faith. We believe in God because God as the creator is present and continues to work within the land, river and sea to give life and hope. This affirmation is the foundation for life. The major problem in theology is the articulation by faith of human history without taking into consideration all the members of the earth's family.

Liberation and integrity of creation

The Bible is the book that affirms the restoration of life from destruction. The verses in the Bible that most strikingly affirm life are concerned with the institution of the Sabbath and Jubilee principles. Jubilee, in the biblical tradition, is an invitation to participate in the dreams and designs of the Divine, to recreate relations among living beings through the restoration and renewal of history. Jubilee epitomizes in historical terms the hope for such an eschatological possibility, creating systems that are free from the potential for exploitation and oppression. Ancient seers introduced the concept of Jubilee through principles of economic, political and social justice within a cosmic framework which inherently negated the marginalization of any living being. To actualize this vision, God revealed himself/herself as the liberator in the exodus event.

More precisely, God was thereby revealed as the God of liberation of the oppressed. 'I am the LORD your God, who has brought you out of the land of Egypt, out of the house of slavery' (Exod. 20.2; Deut. 5.6). Israel as a people came to know God as liberator through the exodus. By delivering the people of Israel from Egyptian bondage and inaugurating the covenant on the basis of that historical event, God was 'revealed as the God of the oppressed, involved in their history, liberating them from human bondage'. In the exodus event, God took the side of the oppressed community, the people who had been denied human dignity and access to the earth's resources.

The Nazareth manifesto of Jesus reaffirmed liberation by proclaiming the year of the Lord's favour. Jesus reiterated the importance of the Jubilee tradition for liberation (Luke 4.18–19). The proclamation of the year of the Lord is a message of liberty to those who have lost their land, personhood or status, letting them know that they may return to their former position and ancestral land; both the rich and poor, master and servant, the empowered and the weak, even nature itself, were to return to their origin. The conflict with Satan and the powers of this world, the condemnation of the rich, the insistence that the kingdom of God is for the poor, and the location of his ministry among the poor for liberation threatened the oppressors, costing Jesus crucifixion. In the absence of a reorganization of life prescribed by the values of Jubilee, a just community is only an empty phrase. The spirituality of Jesus is martyrdom and that is why it is 'costly discipleship'. The resurrection conveys hope in God. That is why Jesus becomes the symbol of struggle for justice for indigenous people. To fight and resist the new empire of the global market and the anti-people development activities of the present day is justified and it is the divine mandate to participate in God's liberative act in history.

Our ecclesial vision

The Church is a house of prayer for all nations, races and languages. There are no barriers, no discrimination in the house of God. Indigenous people, women and persons with disabilities are all invited to celebrate and share their gifts for the common good.

We need to understand the household of God on the basis of the richness of God's creation, as expressed in the plurality of his creation. Attempts to exclude others' forms of expression are a denial of God's richness. No culture, no community is excluded from this God's structure of creation. All are unique in their own ways and, therefore, no one has the right to dominate and oppress another. Life is protected and it can grow to its fullness only by affirming of the beauty of diversity.

Christian missionaries have done immense work for the liberation of indigenous people. Recognizing their genuine interest in the well-being of the oppressed and their commitment to bring to such people the gospel message of salvation, many oppressed people converted to the Christian faith searching for a more dignified life. While acknowledging the many dedicated and selfless works rendered by the missionaries, however, we must also recognize that the Church has been an ally or agent of empire in the marginalization, oppression, exploitation and even obliteration of indigenous peoples' communities. It became the Trojan horse of empire, and to this day continues to be an instrument of subjugation of indigenous peoples' communities. The Church has consistently played her role as a cultural partner in colonization, breaking the will of indigenous people to resist subjugation and domination, and tragically standing in silence in the face of the destruction of our habitat, our livelihood and culture.

Indigenous peoples affirm a people-centred Church, an ecumenical unity, but not a church of power, hierarchy, expansion, extension and conquest. What we envision is a church that respects, recognizes, affirms, supports, promotes, and advocates for us in our struggle for self-identification and self-determination. We envision a Church that goes deeper into indigenous people's experience, not only as an object of study but especially as the *subject* of ecclesiological and theological elaboration.

 SUGGESTED QUESTIONS

1 What are the major features of an indigenous theology in the Asian context?

2 What is the deep connection between the creation and God in the culture of indigenous peoples?

3 What are the major challenges that indigenous people have faced from Christianity? Would you agree that they are threatened communities?

4 How do you understand indigenous people in your own contexts?

5 What are the challenges that their customs and practices pose for their Christian life?

11
Pentecostalism in Asia

Sunder John Boopalan

 Abstract

Boopalan first furnishes here a brief overview of Pentecostalism and its origins, going on to describe Pentecostal developments in various parts of Asia in the twentieth century. He then explicates certain key doctrines of Asian Pentecostalism – namely conversion, baptism and salvation; gifts of the spirit; religious experience, prayer and blessing – while also pointing out other themes in contemporary Asian Pentecostalism: the everyday seeking out of the presence of the supernatural; the mobilization of diverse sections of society; finding the need and meeting it; gospel and culture; ethics and social engagement; personal contact, ecumenism, worship and church life.

 Introduction

People who adhere to forms of charismatic Christianity such as Pentecostalism today comprise almost a quarter of the worldwide Christian population. There has also been a geographical shift in world Christianity, as the regions experiencing the most significant numerical growth in church membership no longer lie in the West. Thanks to this shift, which has been referred to as the 'browning of Christianity' (LaRue, 2009: 18), the numbers of people in the Church in Asia doubled in the twentieth century; some have pointed out that as a result we are moving towards a time when the phrase 'a white Christian' will be an oxymoron. By the dawn of the twenty-first century, Pentecostalism had become the confession of a large majority of Asian Christians and it is now the youngest and fastest growing confession within world Christianity. In this article, I shall define Pentecostalism and trace the origins of this worldwide movement, focusing upon Pentecostal developments in Asia in the twentieth century. Thereafter, I shall consider key doctrines in Pentecostalism and describe various other themes that characterize contemporary Asian Pentecostalism.

Describing Pentecostalism

A distinctive Pentecostal identity is comprised of certain features.

> Pentecostal spirituality emphasizes the importance of intuition and experience whereby the presence of the supernatural is sought out in everyday life; a devotion that places a strong stress on the gifts of the Spirit, which include speaking in tongues and baptism of the Holy Spirit; a firm biblical girding; unwritten liturgy; a theology that is narrated; charismatic leadership with significant lay participation and testimonies; and a focus on the works of the Holy Spirit that is witnessed through healings and signs and wonders.

There are other elements too. The belief that one ought to worship God with one's heart, mind, soul and body means that the whole body is involved in worship. Dreams and visions are often seen as God's communication. Constant prayer, along with prophecy and exorcism, are a daily portion of the Pentecostal experience.

This being so, it is considered by many Pentecostals that 'every generation is the first generation' (Wilson, 1999: 106) in Pentecostalism. Many features of Pentecostalism are thus subject to continual change and depend on the way in which leaders affirm those features.

Though Pentecostalism is largely a phenomenon that emerges from contemporary Protestant Christianity, some scholars have extended the definition to include its influence *within* traditional churches beginning from the 1960s. It has also been said to have influenced certain indigenous movements which do not follow traditional Pentecostalism but have emerged from local revivals (often open to the influence of local expressions of religious experience), or which have become separated from the missions of classical Pentecostalism. These three strands are referred to by some as the 'three waves'.

Origins of Pentecostalism

While the growth of Pentecostalism can legitimately be attributed to the work of the Spirit, commentators have noted that its beginnings may also be traced to nineteenth-century Wesleyan, Reformed and Higher Life holiness circles in the USA, influenced by certain aspects of American and British religious history. Classical or modern Pentecostalism traces its roots to a number of revivals that occurred in the early twentieth century, particularly the Topeka (Kansas) revival of 1900 and those that took place in Azusa Street, Los Angeles in 1906.

Along with this revival, however, there were others. The revival chronicler Edwin Orr speaks of a global 'Fifth General Awakening' between 1900 and 1910, citing as Asian examples the Khasi Revival, the Mukti mission and the Korean Revival. By this time, world Pentecostalism appears to have been Asian in its essence. Azusa Street was thus a sort of prelude to the establishment of a global Pentecostal network. The origin of modern or classical Pentecostalism can therefore no longer be traced solely to the Los Angeles revival of 1906.

Many recent Pentecostal movements in fact are indigenous, meaning that they have emerged from local, autonomous and independent roots, and thus are not bound to the missions of classical Pentecostalism. These indigenous movements tend to be positively open to the inclusion and adaptation of local features and patterns of religious expression, and such movements form a significant element in Asian Pentecostalism.

 ## Asian Pentecostal developments in the twentieth century

In India, Ramabai (1858-1922), a social reformer and advocate of women's rights, and founder of the Mukti mission in Pune, played an important role in the beginnings of Pentecostalism. Inspired by the revivals experienced in the Khasi hills of north-eastern India in 1905, Ramabai saw the happenings that led to the formation of the mission as the work of the Spirit in creating an indigenous Christianity in Asia. An oft-repeated story tells how a girl at the mission was baptized by 'fire'. Falsely thought to have been engulfed by literal flames, she was not however actually on fire but was filled by the Spirit. The confession, repentance and revival that followed stirred the mission into being.

Another prominent character on the Indian scene was Sadhu Sunder Singh (1889-1929), who undertook evangelistic preaching in India and Tibet. Sadhu Sunder Singh was open to visions, healings and miracles, testing these against Christian Scripture. His preaching included arguments which tended to use analogy rather than logic. This use of analogy and narrative is a distinctive feature of Pentecostal preaching even today.

Similar movements in Japan had many Pentecostal features. Kanzo Uchimira (1861-1930), who is known for his 'non-church' (*mu-kyokai*) movement, emphasized that the foundation of church was the subjectivity of faith, a strong Pentecostal feature. He also emphasized that the Church was to be an invisible and entirely spiritual reality and not an institutional one. Alongside this he focused on education, journalism and evangelism. As well as founding the Sapporo Young Men's Christian Association, and protesting against the chemical poisoning that occurred as a result of copper mining in Ashio, he was a strong supporter both of nationalism and

Christianity. Toyohiko Kagawa (1888-1960) laid importance on 'decisions' (the sort of individual decisions that are made after altar calls – where the preacher, during the course of a revival meeting, summons people who would like to submit their lives to Jesus to come forward and do so – are popular in Pentecostal churches). He introduced the idea that the coming of the kingdom could be hastened through the evangelism of believers, a belief of which we find popular traces in many Pentecostal churches.

China is notable for the development of self-propagating, self-governing and self-supporting churches, a concept of many Pentecostal churches today. Also, we find in China movements which were open to healing, prophecy and the realm of signs and wonders; John Sung (1901-44) was responsible for large-scale revivals and thousands of conversions. Wang Ming-Dao (1900-91) was the founder of the Christian Tabernacle, an indigenous church in Beijing. Watchman Nee (1903-72), founder of the 'Little Flocks', challenged the divide between laity and clergy and established a network of consciously non-denominational churches, leading to the emergence of many house church movements in China.

Elsewhere in Asia, Korea witnessed the gifts of the Spirit for the first time through the Great Revival of 1907 in Pyungyang, through which many people became aware of the place of true repentance in Christian life and found Christian living to be characterized by a sense of excitement. This revival in turn inspired a number of other local revivals and also positively energized existing traditional churches. Myanmar has had some notable Pentecostal leaders, most prominent among them Hau Lian Kham (1944-95), a key figure in the movement from the early 1970s. Thanks to his encouragement of lay leadership and inspiration of renewal, he was often called the 'John Wesley of the Zomis', a people among whom he worked. By the year 2000, Protestant Christians had been present in Thailand for 172 years and Pentecostal work had been carried out for 52 years. The country's Pentecostals established their first Bible training institution in 1960, its students going on to found churches in Petchabun and Bangkok.

In the Philippines, since English had become a widely spoken language, the first imports of Pentecostalism were American in origin. The primary carriers, however, were Filipino migrants returning home from the USA, who were, in that sense, indigenously oriented. The Assemblies of God, one of the country's most rapidly growing Pentecostal denominations, today has 1,230 churches.

Pentecostal beginnings in Indonesia can be traced back to 1921. With occurrences such as the rise of Islam and its opposition to foreign dominance, and with the change of leadership in many Protestant churches in the 1930s, Christianity crossed traditional geographical boundaries and churches were established even in predominantly Muslim areas. As a result Christianity became one of the five nationally recognized religions in Indonesia. By the 1930s, Pentecostalism, with its gospel of songs and wonders, mass evangelism, vibrant worship, practical theological education and enthusiastic church planting, witnessed growth throughout the archipelago.

From the time the Gorkha king conquered Nepal until 1951, many restrictions were placed on Christian activity in the country. From that year on, however, converts from bordering areas began to undertake Pentecostal activity. In Nepal, conversion has largely occurred through individual decisions, and no real mass-movement conversions have taken place. In recent times, there has nevertheless been considerable church growth.

The second half of the twentieth century saw the slow but steady growth of Christianity throughout Asia. The Asian churches were seriously affected by the Second World War and subsequent armed conflicts, but despite this a mature evangelicalism emerged and from the 1960s onwards, Asian Protestant Christianity took a turn which by the end of the twentieth century was largely Pentecostal in form.

In Vietnam, Pentecostalism is a relatively new branch of Christianity. However, in recent years, Pentecostalism's theology of empowerment via the Holy Spirit has appealed to many. The movement's influence is said to be so strong that the Assemblies of God reported a growth in numbers from 100 people in 1988 to 16,000 in 1999. Spreading from a few churches in Ho Chi Minh City, by 2001 there were 180 churches in Vietnam. In the light of the government ban on 'Protestant houses', which are termed 'illegal', a key feature of Vietnamese Pentecostalism is the underground church and home-cell group system, along with preaching and evangelism.

Asian Pentecostalism: doctrines

> That Jesus saves (John 3.16), that we are baptized with the Holy Spirit (Acts 2.4), that our bodies are healed (James 5.14–15), and that Jesus is coming again to receive us (1 Thess. 4.16–17), are central themes in Pentecostal doctrine.

Conversion, baptism and salvation

Conviction of sin and individual experience of rebirth are essential elements of Asian Pentecostalism. Awareness of sin is often articulated in testimonies – people's stories of conversion – as the description of a person's sinful life before conversion. Special prayer meetings called tarrying meetings, which are dedicated to the prayer for Spirit baptism, are very widespread. Along with speaking in tongues and Spirit baptism, sanctification is a key Pentecostal doctrine. As with other doctrines, however, there is a diversity of beliefs when it comes to the idea. We can broadly differentiate within it two strands of thought: some believe that sanctification is instant and complete, while others believe that it is a process and that we never achieve totally sinless perfection. What is agreed upon, however, by most Pentecostals is that the idea of holiness is both important and valuable, and that usually it leads to more ethical behaviour in the wider world.

In the first half of the twentieth century, the exterior sins of a holy life were emphasized. Often, sins were associated with the ways of this world and thus holiness entailed a separation from the world in one's external life, often including rejection of leisure, enjoyment and sensual pleasure. But sometimes these ideas had positive social implications. For instance, in India, wearing jewellery indicates one's social status. Since this flaunting of social class was discouraged in Pentecostal churches, the wearing of jewellery was also discouraged.

Within this diversity in the understanding of salvation, there has been an increasing emphasis on its *materiality*, often laying stress on the visibility of one's salvation. For instance, sin is pointed out as corruption; thus the denouncing of sin would also automatically mean the denouncing of corruption in the political and economic spheres of life, thus providing a visible demonstration that one was saved. Sanctification provided evidence of the effect of salvation.

Gifts of the Spirit

Based on 1 Corinthians 12.8–10, most Pentecostals believe in nine distinct gifts of the Spirit: word of knowledge, word of wisdom, discernment of spirits, faith, healing, working of miracles, prophecy, speaking in tongues, and interpretation of tongues.

There is a belief among many Pentecostals in the existence of evil spirits. Some connect evil spirits and demons with the idea of fallen angels. Some also connect evil spirits with those who have suffered an untimely, premature or unlucky death. Illness or misfortune due to the practice of black magic is also acknowledged as a reality, while the view is sometimes held that illness is caused by sins. However, the exercise of discernment is encouraged, so that differentiation may be made between natural causes, evil spirits and black magic. Miracle healing and exorcism thus give Pentecostalism a unique appeal in Asia. These are believed to have greater effect when combined with fasting and prayer, the use of oil that is anointed by praying over it, and the laying on of hands. The emphasis on healing is based on the belief that there is no illness which God cannot heal, and that God wills to restore. Believing that God is the source of all good things, health is received with thanks, both through biblical and medical means.

While the gift of healing is claimed by most Pentecostal leaders, the gift of prophecy is not taken for granted. This being so, many lay people, including women, exercise this gift. There is significant lay participation in the life of the church. For a pastor, however, a direct calling for full-time ministry from God is desirable. In rallies and conventions, altar calls are given whereby people are challenged to commit themselves for full-time ministry.

Religious experience, prayer and blessing

Religious experience, prayer and blessing are important features of Pentecostal spirituality. Some consider speaking in tongues to be the 'initial evidence' of baptism in the Holy Spirit. However, though speaking in tongues is held to be of high importance, other forms of direct experience are also recognized. It is believed that God imparts himself directly to his people through visions, dreams and prophecies. When people narrate their experiences through testimonies, they frequently refer to such manifestations, especially while talking of conversion, Spirit baptism or call to ministry.

Prayer is seen as operating in a realm of power, and is often regarded as having the power to exorcise, and also to be a cause of miracles. This aspect of prayer is further understood when seen in its relation to the manifestation of the Holy Spirit.

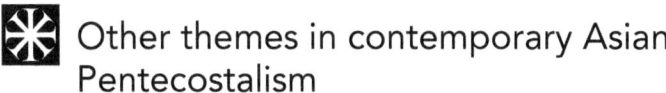 Other themes in contemporary Asian Pentecostalism

The everyday seeking out of the presence of the supernatural

> In contrast with the nineteenth-century view that belief in the spirit world was superstitious or that such a world was imaginary, Asian Pentecostalism has a positive view of the spirit world. Hence, there is a growing acknowledgement by charismatic Christian leaders that the 'demonic' needs to be dealt with.

This often entails exorcism and the control of spirits. In places like Thailand, Pentecostalism represents in some ways a break from indigenous culture, but there is also continuity as far as acknowledgement of the world of the spirits is concerned. The same can be said of Indonesia, where we can trace some elements of animism in Pentecostalism.

The mobilization of diverse sections of society

Asian Pentecostalism has witnessed the embracing of its faith and practice by marginalized sections of the community. In Singapore and Korea, and in many other places, women have played important roles. Moreover, many communities that were traditionally regarded as being of low status (and which in many places continue to be treated that way) have embraced Pentecostalism; for example, the 'lower' castes in India, the Lisu people in Myanmar, and Chinese living overseas in places like Indonesia and Malaysia.

In recent times, however, members of the professional middle classes and some wealthy persons and commercial people have also embraced Pentecostalism. The Trinity Christian Centre in Singapore is a particular example, but there are similar churches in South Korea, India and elsewhere.

We see too a shift in the understanding of Christ; it is a Christ of power rather than the Man of Sorrows who is lifted up.

> Pentecostalism effectively promotes solidarity. When one identifies with a large group, one no longer belongs to the culture of poverty, even though one may still be poor, because the social and psychological heart of the culture of poverty is destroyed.

This sense of worth, solidarity and identification is characteristic of many Asian Pentecostal churches.

Finding the need and meeting it

Once the Bible becomes the central text, many interpretations are possible and the Spirit is not bound. The slogan of one of Pentecostalism's most successful Korean leaders was to 'find need and meet need'. A sense of deliverance is personified in the physical movements and outcries of the people, who often see Pentecostal faith as helping them to move from death to life. This means that Pentecostals are often pragmatic in their approach and proclaim a gospel that addresses practical, everyday concerns like sickness, poverty, loneliness and the work of evil spirits, thus embodying an inherent flexibility in answering fundamental questions raised by the common people.

Gospel and culture

Taiwan, Korea and Japan, among other places, have been influenced by North American culture. But in recent times, the Taiwanese, like the Japanese, have begun to emphasize their own cultural roots. Pentecostal Christianity in these countries can thus be seen as a way of bridging the East and the West. In the Philippines, meanwhile, rural communities were more receptive to Pentecostal preachers; because of the diversity of linguistic and cultural elements that exist in rural contexts, therefore, Pentecostalism in the Philippines tends to be more locally attuned. Also, we see both change and continuity in Pentecostalism. While it resonates with the local 'spirited' world-view, it also breaks with it in its healings, signs and wonders.

Ethics and social engagement

In Thailand, as in Singapore, Christianity's appeal lay in its privileging of responsible living, including the proper treatment of women, the importance of relationships, and a sense of empowerment amid the stress and strain of life. Because Pentecostalism is often involved with the personal and cultural aspects of life, and does not necessarily deal with political action which is connected with violence, the Western academy and media have often overlooked its development, and many facets of Asian Pentecostalism come as a surprise. In general, there is a reluctance within Pentecostalism to engage in politics; this may be understood in the light of influential ideas like 'holiness', where we find an emphasis on personal conversion rather than active engagement in politics.

From the 1980s however there has been increasing social engagement within Pentecostal churches in Asia. Their members feel a need to be good neighbours, called to do something about the physical, spiritual and social needs of the people around them. The Yoido Full Gospel Church in South Korea is a case in point. By 2008, the church had 648 missionaries working in various places, had established seven Bible colleges in places such as Malang in Indonesia, Hong Kong, and Osaka and Tokyo in Japan, as well as one university, and was working extensively in the Third World. Education, health and development programmes are also undertaken by Pentecostal churches in Asia.

Personal contact

Pentecostalism, in many places, primarily spreads through personal contact. There are growing numbers of Pentecostal churches in the Tibeto-Burmese valleys. In places like Nepal, and especially in Kathmandu, dozens of churches are run by the Nepalese themselves. Some examples of such groups are the Nepalese Christian Fellowship, Gospel for Asia and the Baptists of the New Life Mission. Pentecostal churches often function like extended families; their members are in constant touch with each other, and participate mutually in family care and support. Many people thus exercise their social roles within these churches, which give them an identity as people who are needed and valued.

Ecumenism

Various very different groups have joined the Pentecostal movement, as there is no closed membership. Hence, from the beginning, tensions and splits have been a part of the movement. However, Pentecostalism grew in isolation for at least two generations, and from the 1940s its members (who some define as charismatic, but lack speaking in tongues) were accepted within evangelical churches. Some notable Pentecostals were invited by the World Council of Churches to address its members, which has caused some strains in Pentecostals' relationship with evangelicals. Currently, recognizing that some walls are necessary, Pentecostals are ambivalent as to the value of ecumenical relationships.

Worship and church life

Sunday worship is a central feature of Pentecostal piety. Worship often begins with singing, which takes place while the people are filling up the hall or church. The pastor then greets the congregation, after which more songs are sung and prayers of thanksgiving and praise are said. It is noticeable that all members participate in the thanksgiving and all intercede and pray together, partly in tongues. Prophecies and brief exhortations may also be shared. In between further songs, passages from the Bible are read and personal testimonies are given; these highlight how God has worked in the lives of the individuals who speak. The collection is taken and then the sermon begins. Finally some short prayers are offered and the service concludes with a blessing. Often, people go forward to have the pastor's hands laid on them in prayer. Elders appointed for this purpose also pray for the people.

Though the foregoing description may be taken as typical of a Pentecostal service, many variations may be found; often the leader's charisma is acknowledged and the congregation is open to changes in worship initiated by the pastor or leader. Adaptation of other churches' practices happens frequently in Asian Pentecostalism. For instance, the prayer cells idea, patterned on those of Yongi Cho in South Korea, is now a central feature in many Asian Pentecostal churches.

Much importance is given to thanksgiving and praise, and the atmosphere of free worship is often filled with emotional expression as people sense the nearness of God. This ecstatic and liberating experience in the presence of God is a key feature of Pentecostalism. The giving of testimonies is marked by the narration of experiences of healing or deliverance from situations of need and anxiety. There is active lay participation, which facilitates a mutual concern for each participant's lot. The sermon is central and takes up a significant portion of time in the service. The pastor's charisma, oratory skills and elements of empathy and rhetoric are greatly valued.

A Pentecostal enters the place of worship in submission and leaves with a mission. On total surrender, individuals are pressed by the Spirit to communicate the blessings they have received to the larger world outside. This overflow is proclaimed with enthusiasm and the cure and freedom is announced; a cure from the things that hold one down, and freedom from alcoholism, hate, disbelief and imposed helplessness.

Pentecostal commentators relate the charismatic experience to play, in that people freely choose to let go, in a sense, of ordinary and mundane ways of living in order to enter into a world of freedom energized by the Spirit for spontaneous relationships and wholehearted mission. What is important in this aspect of Pentecostalism is that such play is not a retreat from the world, but rather draws energy in and from the Spirit so as to be better able to deal with the challenges of everyday living.

In conclusion: moving between the word and Spirit, structure and freedom

The various occurrences and events that have centred around Pentecostalism have been referred to by many names. Asian Pentecostalism, in particular, has been termed the awakening of the 'rest' of global society; others have called it the largest global shift in world Christianity; still others have pointed out that in addition to this geographical shift, it is also a theological shift.

Pentecostals demonstrate an openness to the Holy Spirit that at times indicates a *moving beyond* the realm of positivistic rationality. As pointed out by an Asian Pentecostal leader, this understanding of Christian guidance does not deny the role of the unconscious but rather seeks to testify that the Holy Spirit sanctifies not just humanity's conscious, but also the unconscious and the subconscious.

While there is a broad Pentecostal consensus on the importance and significance of the charismata in the life of the Church, there is also substantial diversity beyond this recognition. Asian Pentecostalism is an example of this diversity. The distinctive scene in Asia is an expression of Pentecostalism's diversity and its multiple expressions. When it comes to Asia, even those considered to be classical Pentecostal churches reflect a great diversity in both beliefs and practices compared to their Western counterparts. The range of Pentecostal phenomena that comes under the focus of Asian churches is broader. Because it is believed that the Holy Spirit calls and gifts individual believers as distinct from the institutions they are affiliated to, Pentecostalism in Asia has taken on a wide variety of forms according to the context in which it becomes established.

 SUGGESTED QUESTIONS

1 What is Pentecostalism? What are the origins of Pentecostalism?

2 What are the main forms of Pentecostalism in Asia? How are they similar to forms of Pentecostalism in your own context?

3 Discuss some key doctrines of Pentecostalism in Asia. Are these doctrines important in your own church tradition and context? Compare and contrast.

Part 4
Worms'-eye views of the furrows

12
Minjung theology: whose voice, for whom?

Sebastian Kim

 Abstract

Kim traces the origins of the Minjung movement in the context of the changing politics of the Korean economy. As a contextual theology designed to address the problems of poverty, Minjung theology protested against both the unjust economic system in Korea and the country's conservative fundamentalist theology. Furthermore, it articulated alternative images of Jesus as Minjung and viewed the Minjung or the poor masses as the subjects of history. Kim goes on to address a few pertinent questions concerning the methodology of Minjung theology. First, is Minjung theology by or of the Minjung themselves or is it a theology by elites for the Minjung? And second, who are the Minjung in contemporary Korea today and how do they see themselves? He uses these questions to foreground discussions on the significance and relevance of Minjung theology today.

 The Minjung movement

The Minjung movement in South Korea exploded in Korean politics when Jun Tae-Il set himself on fire on 13 November 1970 as his protest against the exploitation of fellow factory workers. The incident shook the country and drew attention to the problem of the *Jaebul* or family-run mega-companies which, encouraged by government, rose rapidly during the 1960s and 1970s to dominate the Korean economy.

In 1973, some Christian leaders challenged the government and the capitalist market economy by signing 'The Korean Christian Manifesto', which declared that God is on the side of the poor and the oppressed. However, the majority of church leaders saw the problem as simply a matter of the 'process' of development and concentrated in their emphasis on church growth. In this period, the *Jaebul* and mega-churches rose in parallel and the church leadership believed the growth of the Christian population and the growth of the national economy went hand-in-hand. There was a need for a new theological paradigm to meet the need of the urban poor whose poverty, some Christian intellectuals stressed, was not due to their own lack of industry but because they were victims of the highly competitive capitalist market.

> Minjung theology developed into a major contextual theology intended to address the problems of the poor and the exploited. It has employed socio-political tools developed in the West and articulated in Latin America and was formulated in the 1970s as a protest theology against the unjust system of modern and divided Korea on the one hand, and against conservative fundamentalist theologies on the other.

In 1975, Suh Nam-Dong, among the most well-known of Minjung theologians, presented his thesis that Jesus identified with the poor, the sick and the oppressed and that the gospel of Jesus is the gospel of salvation and liberation. The gospel is the struggle against evil powers and liberation is not individual or spiritual but rather communal and political. Suh systematized his Minjung theology in the following years, seeing the Minjung as the subjects of history and dealing with *han* or deep despair, anger and sadness as the key theme for theology in the Korean context. Ahn Byung-Mu, another well-known Minjung theologian, asserted that Jesus identified in such a way that Jesus *is* Minjung and Minjung *is* Jesus as he shared his life with the Minjung, and that the event of the Cross is the climax of the suffering of the Minjung. Therefore the presence of Christ is not when the word is preached nor when the sacrament is conducted but when we participate with or in the suffering of the Minjung. Jesus is God becoming flesh and body, which means material being and reality in everyday life. He regarded the concept of a worshipping community as a later development of what began as a 'food community', that is a community sharing food.

Minjung theologians captured the people's imagination and brought the issue of poverty and exploitation into the Church. In their interpretation the suffering of the poor and the exploited is not individualized but is 'relational', it is the result of the greediness of some others and the unjust system of modern capitalism. Therefore, Minjung theologians' main concern is to deal with social process and the system which prevents the Minjung from coming out of their misery. In this respect, Minjung theologians' focus is on what is anti-Minjung rather than with the Minjung themselves.

Minjung theology has made an important contribution to the Korean Church and society through its emphasis on liberation and justice, and by showing the poor and the oppressed that they are not or should not be the objects of exploitation and that their protest was a legitimate one. However, questions have been raised about the methodology of Minjung theology in two areas: Whose voice? And for whom? That is, whether Minjung theology is by the Minjung or of the Minjung or whether it is a theology by elites for the Minjung? And, second, who are the Minjung in contemporary Korea and how do they see themselves? Are they only a conceptual group which is created by theologians for the purpose of their argument?

On the question of the identity of Minjung theologians, and therefore of Minjung theology itself, the answer is positive. Though most of them are intellectuals and not from a Minjung background, Minjung theologians *did* identify themselves with Minjung by participating in suffering with them. Because of their identification with Jesus and the Minjung in their theology, they made themselves vulnerable, went to prison and went through economic hardship. In this way they suffered with the Minjung and so the Minjung theologians, at least in the first generation in the 1970s, *became* Minjung. Their theology was the outcome of their struggle as Minjung against their oppressors. Therefore, Minjung theology has a legitimate place in the life of Korean people as *of* the Minjung and thus gives self-identity to the Minjung.

When we come to the second generation of Minjung theologians in the 1980s, this claim is not so firmly founded. Particularly after the Kwangju massacre in 1980 by a military-backed government, Minjung theologians shifted their attention from the socio-economic problem of poor workers and farmers to ideological issues, taking a socialist-communist line. The first generation had had the support of the 'mass' of workers and farmers over against the employers and land owners but the second generation had only minority support because of their use of Marxist ideology in their theologizing. This created a large gap between the Minjung who were not prepared to be seen as on the side of North Korea, which is a communist state, and those theologians for whom Minjung theology was part of their ideological struggle.

The second question of the identity of the Minjung is a more difficult one. The term *minjung*, which is a Chinese word for ordinary people or citizens, is quite a new and unfamiliar one for contemporary South Koreans. In addition, people find it difficult to identify themselves with this heavily loaded term without definite or immediate benefits associated with it. In a rapidly changing society like contemporary Korea, people are not prepared to commit themselves to such a static concept as Minjung and for the cause of the Minjung, but in contrast, they rather wish to rise out of the Minjung. Unlike black theology, feminist theology and Dalit theology, Minjung theologians have had difficulties equating this term with a concrete and tangible group, as shown by the number of articles devoted to defining the Minjung.

Though Latin American liberation theology made the point that the poor and the oppressed are the ones who need to be liberated, Minjung theology moves beyond this and asserts that the Minjung are the subjects of this liberation as well as the subjects of the history and the culture of their particular contexts.

> The identity of the Minjung has been vital to Minjung theology, and this was expressed as in the relationship between Jesus and the Minjung: Jesus is the Minjung and the Minjung is Jesus.

Minjung theologians asserted that the Minjung has to be understood as an experiential entity identified with the 'event' of Jesus, especially his passion. The 'Minjung as Jesus' does not mean that they are him in an ontological sense, but that they are experiencing the Jesus event and therefore able to be in Jesus and be part of his mission in this world.

The question of the identity of the Minjung is a crucial one. The challenge faced by Minjung theology is to extend the identity of the Minjung beyond the particular Korean context to create Minjung theologies (plural). These continue to be theologies *of Minjung by Minjung*. The Minjung methodology is preserved but the subjects of theologizing change to include, for example, foreign factory workers in Korea, the people of North Korea, and oppressed groups in other parts of the world. The definition of the Minjung then becomes the starting point for theology. Otherwise Minjung theology will remain a particular theology developed in the Korean context of the 1970s and 1980s. Whatever happens, Minjung theology has made a significant contribution to the Korean church and to wider theological discourse of seeing the Minjung as the *subjects* of theologizing, and this affirmation in itself has been the gospel to those struggling to see God's presence in their midst.

 SUGGESTED QUESTIONS

1 How did Minjung theology originate?

2 What are the major features of the theological constructions of Suh Nam-Dong and Ahn Byung-Mu?

3 Do you agree that Minjung theology is a theology of the poor? Are there any similar theologies in your context which take the situation of the poor seriously?

13
Devious devotion to Christ: the making of Indian Christologies

Joseph Prabhakar Dayam

 Abstract

Dayam here helps us to understand how Christian theologians in the religiously pluralistic context of India sought to contextualize Christ by treading what he calls a 'deviant path'. He focuses his attention on the Christological constructions of two important strands of Indian Christian theology, namely Vedic theology and Rethinking Christianity, choosing one representative from each of these strands. While the representative of Vedic theology, Krishna Mohan Banerjea, draws parallels between Vedic Hinduism and Christianity using as a basis the centrality of sacrifice, the representative of Rethinking Christianity, Pandipeddi Chenchiah, focuses on the significance and meaning of Jesus' personality.

 Introduction

Indian Christian theologians, while retaining the centrality of Christ in their attempts to contextually make sense of the Christian gospel, have sought a new language and employed diverse paradigms in understanding the meaning and significance of Christ. In so doing they have on the one hand *devoted themselves* to Christ and on the other *resisted the colonial interpretations* of Christ and offered their own Christologies by treading a deviant path. In this essay I will examine how Christ is understood within two Indian theological movements, namely Vedic theology and Rethinking Christianity theology. In so doing I will take one representative from each movement and attempt to discern the theologies that operated in the work of each in imagining Indian Christologies.

The 'Vedic theology' of Krishna Mohan Banerjea: Christ as the *Prajāpati* and his death as the primordial sacrifice

The interaction of cultural, economic and political forces during the British Raj in India brought about the early nineteenth-century movement known as the Bengal Renaissance. One aspect of such interaction was the encounter between Christianity and Hinduism. 'This encounter manifested itself in different ways – conflict, adjustment, reconciliation, revival and re-interpretation' (Philip, 1982: 1). All religious and secular movements of that time in Bengal in some way or other reacted to the Christian challenge, resulting in a situation of conflict between respect for Christ and antipathy to Christian missionary endeavour, and between modernity and tradition.

> From within the Church, the reaction to Hindu tradition expressed itself in two ways. There was an aggressive resentment of Hinduism in certain sections and there were also attempts made to establish a positive and creative relationship between Christianity and Hinduism.

The encounter of Christianity and Hinduism occasioned the publication of a large number of Christian apologetic writings. Those apologetics produced by the Indians mark the beginning of indigenous theological thinking among Protestants in India, and Krishna Mohan Banerjea was the outstanding apologist of that period. Banerjea constantly argued for the claims of Christianity. He considered Christianity as a divine revelation which was at the same time also rational, and criticized Hindu philosophy for being irrational. Being an apologist he maintained that the book of revelation is not contrary to the book of nature. In his opinion, the Vedas had originally contained revelation but were later distorted.

Though Banerjea was at first extremely critical of Hinduism, after 1865 his approach changed. His works *The Arian Witness* (1880) and *The Relation Between Christianity and Hinduism* (1881) concern themselves with establishing a positive relationship between the two religions. In his revised view, Christianity does not displace Vedic religion but in some essential way fulfils it. It is this understanding that befits the naming of his theology as 'Vedic theology' (Boyd, 1975: 65). In his view, Vedic literature bears witness to the truth of the Bible; the Brahminical sutras and the practices of sacrifice prefigure the vicarious atonement of Christ and foreshadow the primitive revelation of the future saviour.

For Banerjea, the 'essence' of Christianity lies in its belief in the atoning sacrifice of Christ understood as vicarious substitution; 'the sacrifice of the Lamb slain from the foundation of the world' is the cornerstone of the Christian faith.

> Though Christianity has its variations in the form of several denominations, its core for Banerjea lies in the assertion of the scheme of reconciliation between God and the world through the meritorious sacrifice of Christ (Banerjea, 1881: 182).

The seed of the woman is the Lamb slain from the foundation of the world. 'His sacrifice, though accomplished in time, was commemorated and typified from the beginning.' The recorded instances of Old Testament sacrifice were 'consequent on the institution of such sacrifices from the beginning under divine direction, at once commemorative and prefigurative of the great Sacrifice of the Lamb slain from the foundation of the world' (Banerjea, 1881: 90).

The sacrifices offered by Abel, Noah and Job are such anticipations of the one that is to come. Though the blood of bulls or lambs will not take away the sin of humankind, they were instituted as 'a fore-shadowing of the truly saving sacrifice' (Banerjea, 1880: 90, 91).

Similarly, Banerjea suggests, sacrifice is at the core of Hinduism, particularly of Vedic Hinduism as he perceived it. Concerning sacrifice, the 'Arian Witness' (by this he means the Vedic Hindu witness) makes the following assertions:

> One, the sacrifice is initiated by *Purusa* or *Prajāpati*, the Lord, or rather the *preserver* of the creation as he offered himself as sacrifice for the welfare of *devas*, and those were born as 'mortals' but had attained to immortality in heaven.
>
> Two, Sacrifice was the authorized means for the remission of sins. It is by offering sacrifices, the *Devas*, who were originally men attained celestial bliss.
>
> Three, the idea of the Seed of Woman bruising the head of the serpent is not alien to the Arian religious heritage. 'He knew of "the great dragon" that old serpent, called the Devil and Satan whose subjugation and destruction has always been the great struggle of life with God-fearing men.'
>
> Four, The Seed of Woman, who is the Christ, finds his counterpart in the Vedic understanding of *Prajāpati*. This Hindu-Christian acknowledgement of Christ as the *Prajāpati*, will find endorsement with the Vedic Visionaries, the primitive ancestors of Hindu faith, if they return back to life.
>
> (Banerjea, 1880: 94, 95)

Banerjea, through his study of the Vedas and Upanishads, finds that the idea of the sacrifice of a divine person is not an isolated one but finds expression in various passages, directly and indirectly. It is this idea that gives significance to the frequent Vedic exhortation to engage in the performance of *Yajna* (sacrifice). According to Banerjea, this idea is personified in *Prajāpati*.

> For Banerjea, this Vedic vision or the ideal of the self-sacrifice of *Prajāpati* found its correlation in the person of Christ.

He writes,

> The self-sacrifice of *Prajāpati*, curiously resembles the Biblical description of Christ as God and man, our very Emmanuel, mortal and immortal, who 'hath given Himself for us, an offering and a sacrifice to God for a sweet smelling savor,' of whom all previous sacrifices were but figures and reflections, who by His sacrifice or death hath 'vanquished death, and brought life and immortality to light through the Gospel.' (Banerjea, 1880: 193)

This identification of *Prajāpati* is not just a coincidental textual occurrence but is singularly fulfilled in the person and his atoning sacrifice. This fulfilment could be traced in his name, Jesus, and in his death and resurrection. The word *Prajāpati* is a derivative of two Sanskrit words, *Prajā* and *Pati*, which mean 'people' and 'Lord' respectively. Therefore *Prajāpati* means the Lord of people or the Lord of creatures. But it also means 'the supporter, feeder and deliverer of his creatures' (Banerjea, 1880: 194). The name Jesus implies a similar meaning, as the saviour or deliverer. This name is given to him to indicate that he would save his people from their sins. Therefore the name *Prajāpati* uniquely corresponds to the name of Jesus, who uniquely qualifies for the appellation *Prajāpati*. Banerjea further writes:

> Not a single character in the Hindu pantheon, or in the pantheon of any other nation, has claimed the position of one who offered himself as a sacrifice for the benefit of humanity. There is, as all educated persons must know, only one historical person, Jesus of Nazareth, whose name and position corresponds to that of the Vedic ideal – one mortal and immortal, who sacrificed himself for the (hu)mankind. (Banerjea, 1880: 195)

Since Christ perfectly and uniquely fits the appellation of *Prajāpati*, the Vedic ideal, Banerjea suggests that the death of Christ is a symbol of the primordial ideal of sacrifice symbolized in *Prajāpati*, or the *Purusa*.

Christology from the Madras Rethinking Christianity group

The Madras Rethinking Christianity group was one of the most prominent among the early twentieth-century theological movements in India that shaped consequent theological articulations both in terms of content and method. The group got its name as a result of its responses to Hendrik Kraemer's *The Christian Message in a Non-Christian World*, when in preparation for the World Missionary Conference at Tambaram in 1938 it published a book with the title *Rethinking Christianity in India*. The contributors to this book included among others Pandipeddi Chenchiah and Vengal Chakkarai. Contesting Kraemer's idea about the discontinuity between Christianity and Hinduism, the writers insisted on the value of Hinduism as a 'spiritual eye' enabling the recognition of Jesus and as 'the spiritual mother' who teaches her children spiritual discernment (Jathanna, 1981: 360). Challenging the exclusivist position of Kraemer, these theologians argued for the permeation of Christianity into Hindu society, a gradual infusion of Hinduism by Christian ideals and Christian life without disrupting the identity and integrity of Hinduism (Grafe, 1990: 172).

The contributions of the Madras Rethinking Christianity group could be discerned in the following areas:

- arguing for a movement from translation to construction of theology;
- reconsidering the sources of authority for Indian Christian theology;
- reclaiming the religious heritage of converts to Christianity;
- offering a distinctively Indian Christology.

Chenchiah's Christological contribution

In the words of Robin Boyd, Pandipeddi Chenchiah is 'one of the most striking and original figures in the history of Indian Christian theology' (Boyd, 1975: 144). Christology occupies the central place in Chenchiah's theology. His view of Christianity's relationship with other religions is derived from his radical Christocentric position. Christology is for Chenchiah the point of departure for Christian theology. For him Christology primarily has to do with the significance and meaning of Jesus' personality. The fact of Christ precedes the function of Christ and the latter is dependent on the former. As O. V. Jathanna observes, 'Chenchiah sees Jesus's significance more in onto-logical-metaphysical terms than in functionalistic terms, and seeks to emphasize Jesus's metaphysical and cosmic importance' (Jathanna, 1981: 387). Chenchiah writes, 'In seeking the elucidation of Jesus in terms of His function, we miss the deeper meaning of the fact of Jesus in the context of the creative flow of existence. Jesus saves, but he does this by virtue of the status and constitution of His Being i.e., by His Sonship' (Thangasamy, 1966: 102).

Chenchiah was impelled to formulate his Christological ideas by his evangelistic and theological concerns to understand the uniqueness of Christ and to present Christ meaningfully to Hindus. He sought to answer the question, wherein does the uniqueness of Christ lie? Chenchiah felt that traditional interpretations of Christ failed to make Christ speak to Indian sensibilities and failed to capture the newness of Christ to Indian minds.

> For Chenchiah the uniqueness of Christ lies 'in the "fact" that in Jesus humanity has witnessed the birth of a New Man as the result of God's new creative effort, and the arrival of New Spirit, the Holy Spirit, into the world' (Jathanna, 1981: 389).

To capture the uniqueness of Christ Chenchiah finds the evolutionary framework of 'the cosmic evolution of life' helpful because it provides a way by which the newness of 'the new' can be understood on its own terms and not in terms of the past. His understanding of evolution is that it is not atheistic, naturalistic and mechanical but revolutionary. Chenchiah contends that God's revelation is present in creation. He talks of the creation as primary revelation and assigns to Scripture the status of secondary revelation. 'Revelation is not, as Christians and Hindus believe, the speech or the word of God. It is the creation' (Thangasamy, 1966: 104). He sees divine revelation in the revolutions that occur in creation. Creation is evolution that is punctuated at critical stages by revolution. Jesus is not only the latest revolution in the creative process but also perhaps the last. In the birth of Jesus, Spirit entered creation by becoming flesh. The birth, life, death and resurrection of Jesus suggest a new current of life that entered the creative process (Thangasamy, 1966: 116–21). He writes:

> Jesus is the latest revolution in the creative process. Placed alongside the earlier terms of creative atom, cell, man – matter, life, soul – Jesus marks the addition of new creative power, the potentiality of new creative order. As Life is to matter, the soul is to life, so is Jesus to man. He is the Son of Man – the child of humanity – a diversion of human stream to a higher level. Jesus is the vertical descent of spirit into the horizontal stream of creation which, like the freshness comes from on high, flows into the streams and carries it onward. Man is not the last and highest term of creation. The process of creation finds its crown and culmination in Jesus. Jesus is the new Man – the dream of mankind come into life. He is more than a Redeemer, Messiah, and Teacher. He is the prototype, a new creation, the first of a new race of children of God. He is the latest term of creative process and may be the last. (Thangasamy, 1966: 116)

For Chenchiah it is the immanence of God that is important. By turning Jesus into God we are trying to make of him what he resisted becoming. In the incarnation, Jesus wanted to step out of God and became human. Jesus is not God the absolute but God standing in relation to the (hu)man (Thangasamy, 1966: 90).

The emphasis on the person of Jesus as the 'new (hu)Man' and the secondary place assigned to the function of Christ naturally leads Chenchiah to question the traditional way of seeing the cross of Christ as the key in formulating Christology. Therefore he finds it problematic to reduce the work of Christ to any theory of reconciliation (Thangasamy, 1966: 93). Chenchiah sought to contest any attempt to explain the death of Christ by using language from the court and the temple. The work of Christ lies in taking us beyond these human institutions to new possibilities opened to creation in the event of his incarnation.

Restricting the work of Christ to reconciliation in terms of justification by faith resulted in the view that the ultimate effect of that work was to restore humanity to its 'original' condition or to its primal stage before the fall. In this view, the work of Christ can be to provide only a new start for life, but not its positive content. Chenchiah's concern was to go beyond this new start and seek an advance for human beings beyond it. The incarnation of Christ needs to point to new possibilities. According to Chenchiah, Barth's view of incarnation (as he understood it from Barth's early writings and those of Kraemer) is as the advent of the incognito God. The idea that God touched the world as a tangent touches the circle – touching without touching – is neither original nor sufficient. It is in no way different from the concept of incarnation in Hinduism. In Hinduism God incarnates whenever the constitution of the world is threatened. His purpose is not to dwell with us always but 'to restore the mechanisms of life to its original condition' (Thangasamy, 1966: 94). The Christian conception of incarnation needs to be more than this:

> The fact of Christ is the birth of a new order in creation. It is the emergence of life – not bound by Karma of man, not tainted by sin, not humbled by death, of man triumphant, glorious, partaking the immortal nature of God, of the birth of a new race in the creation of sons of God. If Jesus is not the incarnation of this, what else could he be? A mere visitor from heaven who, moved by his love, made a supreme sacrifice and then went away to his place at the right hand of God? Is he not Immanuel, God permanently residing in the creation – the answer to the prayer of man to transcend his destiny? If the incarnation is the answer to our ambition and not to our infirmities – then humanity has a future, a new future more in accord with its aspirations.
>
> (Thangasamy, 1966: 94, 95)

For Chenchiah, Jesus brought in a new possibility in human history, the possibility of human beings entering a new stage – the possibility of humans becoming the children of God. 'Children of God' is not just an identity but an inner reality. This possibility is not something out there in the eschaton but here and now. He writes:

> Jesus is not the window through which we behold the new Sons of Man as in a vision. He is the Son of God and we can be and ought to be sons of God now and here – not in the far-off future. I am afraid this conception of the Kingdom of God not as a development of the world order but as something which will descend from heaven when Christ comes, seems to be not only a primary heresy but also a present tragedy. It has postponed our appropriation of Jesus as a present reality. This converts Christianity into a religion of repentance, not a rebirth. To be born again is Christianity and the new-born is the son of God and the order he evolves the Kingdom of God. India longs to learn the secrets of this new birth which transcends Karma. If we can not give it, we are offering sand and ashes calling it loudly divine food. (Thangasamy, 1966: 95)

Jesus as the Son of Man continues his incarnation and is immanently present through his resurrection as the Spirit that empowers humans. Although it is important to talk about God in terms of transcendence, there can be no justification in talking of the transcendence of Jesus.

> The incarnation has its spearhead towards creation. To turn it around and make it face heaven is to reverse its purpose. Confusion is due to the use of the word incarnation – an unbiblical term. In the company of Jesus we do not feel the gulf that separates God from man. We feel he is the bridge, the hyphen that

unites God and men. His own consciousness reveals the total lack of this sense of separation and his teachings do not emphasize the awful gulf between God and humans. Else, Our Lord would not have bid us to be perfect like God. His desire to be like God was the sin of Adam but the virtue of the Christian. The emphasis on 'the son' in the 'Son of God' and the 'Son of Man' is illuminating. Jesus is not God and is not (hu)Man, but is the Son of God and the Son of man. The word 'Son' indicates the measure of unity – something less than complete identity with God but something more than difference in category – between God, Jesus, and the Christian. God is God. (hu)Man is (hu)Man. The twain have met in Jesus: not merely met, but fused and mingled into one. Hinduism always longed for a state in which one could say as Jesus did, 'I and my father are one' – which was our Lord's affirmation of the Brahma Vakya *Aham Brahmasmi* . . . in Jesus it was, for the first time in history, an accomplished reality, not an unrealized aspiration. . . . The incarnation is as much what humans are to become as what God has become. (Thangasamy, 1966: 96)

Conclusion

Indian Christian theologians' utter devotion to Christ propelled them to imagine Christ based on foundations that are Indian and aspirations that are felt within the Indian spiritual quest. In their Christologies these theologians deviated from the traditional formulations of the Christian councils and creeds and ventured to make a sense of Christ's meaning and significance forged in Indian crucibles. While Banerjea tried to understand the person of Christ by explicating the work of Christ as *Prajāpati*, Chenchiah's primary concern was to locate his significance for us in Jesus' being. These Christologies give us an idea of the various ingenious ways through which Indian Christian theologians not only brought Hindu concepts and biblical ideas together (Banerjea) but also, by focusing on the person of Jesus and understanding Christ in relation to the biblical concept of the new creation (Chenchiah), discerned and derived important directions for meaningful Christian living in creative fidelity to the life and personality of Jesus Christ.

 SUGGESTED QUESTIONS

1 What were the main reasons for the emergence of Indian Christian Christologies?

2 What was the main focus of Chenchiah's Christological articulation? Do you agree with Chenchiah's emphasis on the personality of Jesus in the articulation of Christology?

3 Do you find resonances between the Christological articulations of Krishna Mohan Banerjea and Christologies in your own context?

14
Contextual Christian theologies in China prior to 1950

Lawrence Braschi

 Abstract

In this chapter Braschi presents a broad picture of the development of contextual Christian theologies in China before the rise of the Chinese Communist Party in 1949, focusing on the contributions made by Chinese Christians and foreign missionaries. While early Nestorian and Catholic theologies in China took the form of hymns, prayers, liturgies and homilies, later missionary theologies focused on the relations between Chinese tradition and issues surrounding Christian participation in traditional rites and Confucianism. Braschi points out that the Protestant missionary theologies of the nineteenth and twentieth centuries focused on biblical translation and conversion, whereas the Protestant Chinese Christian theology of the twentieth century focused on the indigenization of Chinese Christian theology.

 Introduction

Chinese Christianity prior to 1950 was dominated by its foreign and minority status.

> Like the theologies of other Christian minority movements around the world, Christian theology in China has been less concerned with metaphysics than morality, more concerned with indigenization than systematization.

The 'foreign' nature of Christian theology in China has frequently led to tension with and opposition from Chinese traditions and culture, both within and outside the Chinese churches. In the best cases such tension has led to considerable creativity, which remains the foundation for indigenous Chinese theology today. In other cases, imposed foreign conceptions and ecclesial hierarchies led to the stifling of indigenous expressions of Christianity. Such expressions only fully emerged after foreign missionary involvement was cut off by the rise of the Chinese Communist Party to power in 1949. This survey will identify some of the distinctively contextual contributions made by Chinese Christians and foreign missionaries up until that defining moment.

'Nestorian' and Catholic theologies in China

The bulk of Chinese Christian theological reflection during the 'first wave' of Christian activity in China was in the form of hymns, prayers, liturgies and homilies. Such *theologia prima* have been found in the walled-up cave libraries at Dunhuang, dating from the fourth to the twelfth centuries CE, and provide so far the earliest documentation we have of Chinese Christianity. Longer *sutras* on monotheism, almsgiving and the Messiah are preceded by sections on subjects such as the divine right of emperors. Translations of Syriac Christian hymns and liturgies also utilized Daoist and Buddhist religious loan words to create distinctively Chinese Christian variants. The famous 'Nestorian stele' relates the providential history of the 'luminous teaching' in China, and reveals the efforts of its leading Syrian monks to contextualize Trinitarian ideas and iconography within the religious environment of eighth-century China. It culminates with the provocative statement that this foreign religion contains the best understanding of the universe's underlying principle, the *dao*. Subsequent translations of Buddhist texts written between the ninth and fourteenth centuries reveal Christian (and Manichaean) influences, showing the cross-pollination of theological languages in 'Chinese' Central Asia during the Mongol period. Christian theological writing in China largely disappeared following successive imperial proscriptions of foreign religions and the realignment of the Syriac Christian heartlands to Islam.

Later missionaries from Central Asia, the Middle East and Europe were confronted with a complex, self-sufficient and (predominantly) self-assured Chinese cultural and religious world.

> Broad theological conversations between these missionaries, Chinese Christian converts and other Chinese dialogue partners may be summarized in terms of two specific issues: first, whether Chinese traditions contained a pre-Christian revelation of God and, if so, which Chinese terms most clearly expressed it; second, whether Chinese Christian converts could, in all conscience, participate in traditional rites and festivals in honour of family ancestors and Confucius.

The celebrated Italian Jesuit missionary Matteo Ricci (1552–1610) spent nearly thirty years in China and developed an influential model of accommodation to parts of the Chinese tradition. His introduction to Christian teaching, *The True Meaning of the Lord of Heaven* (*Tianzhu shiyi*), first published in 1603, utilizes the familiar Chinese genre of a dialogue, combining arguments from natural theology with a selective interpretation of Confucian classical texts. His last chapter explains the incarnation of Jesus Christ as the final revelation of the same Lord of Heaven (*Tianzhu*) found in the Confucian canon. Ricci's espousal of the language of classical Confucianism was justified on the supposed purity of ancient Chinese monotheism, prior to the intervention of later Daoist and Buddhist accretions.

In the writings of the Catholic convert Yang Tingyun (1562–1627), we have a detailed exegesis of Ricci's synthesis from a scholarly Chinese perspective. Yang undertook a close Confucian-Christian dialogue, focused on how Christian teaching validated the 'original transmission' of the Confucian canon. In this way Christianity could bolster Confucian ethical teachings with a religious understanding of life, death, God and spirit. Yang and other Confucian converts amplified Ricci's criticism of Buddhist terminology, particularly its conceptions of the soul, hell and human nature.

Some prominent Chinese scholarly converts also suggested that the Jesuits accept classical Chinese expressions as equivalents for the biblical relative terms for God, namely *tian* (heaven) and *shangdi* (lord on high).

The Jesuits generally adopted a scholarly rather than a distinctly religious identity, and came to be described by sympathetic Chinese as 'Western Confucians'. By contrast, mendicant missionaries and their converts in China from the mid-seventeenth century concentrated on direct evangelization. These missionaries criticized the Jesuits' habit of downplaying Jesus' identification with criminals at his crucifixion, aware as they were of the offence it gave to Chinese sensibilities. The friars' missions were aimed toward humbler and poorer Chinese in the coastal provinces, whom they organized into confraternities. The mendicants' post-Tridentine theology opposed accommodations with non-Catholic teaching or ritual, and Franciscan and Dominican priests led the opposition to converts' participation in Chinese rites. This 'rites controversy' erupted when the French vicar-apostolic for Southern China banned all converts from participating in the Confucian rites. The Jesuits appealed to the Manchu Kangxi emperor to argue that the rites had a civil rather than religious significance, but the prohibitions were upheld by the Vatican. This controversy contributed to the eventual proscription of Christianity as a heterodox and harmful teaching in 1724.

Protestant missionary theologies in the nineteenth and twentieth centuries

Protestant missionaries arrived on the periphery of China at the beginning of the nineteenth century, and for the first fifty years were confined to working only in the Chinese 'treaty ports' and diaspora. Partly as a result, the principal theological contribution of the first generation of Protestant converts and missionaries was the translation of the Bible into Chinese, a project particularly associated with Robert Morrison (1782–1834). In an attempt to create a standard theological vocabulary, later Protestant missionaries revisited the 'interminable controversy' over the appropriate Chinese terms for God. Even after thirty years of preparatory work, the Christian Union Version (1919) was published in two separate editions, each using one of the opposing terms *shen* (which roughly meant 'god' or 'spirit' and had polytheistic connotations) and *shangdi* (which meant 'Sovereign on high'). Another outcome of the Protestant emphasis on biblical translation was to be the range of versions in vernacular and 'tribal' languages which were published over the next several decades, entirely without the disputes associated with the Chinese language translations.

Early evangelical missionaries such as the Moravian Karl Gützlaff (1803–51) and the English Methodist James Hudson Taylor (1832–1905) were highly impressed by the sheer number of the 'heathen masses' in China. Both came to emphasize the importance of extensive travel by Chinese evangelists and foreign missionaries, with the aim of rapid conversion, and gave less emphasis to theological adaptation or church-building, trusting that the Holy Spirit would guide believing converts. Convinced of the mystical union of Christ and the believer, Taylor created an incarnational 'fellowship', the China Inland Mission (CIM), whose members' aim would be to share the common life of the Chinese. As the first of the 'faith missions', the CIM was in part a theological response to the scale of the task of 'converting China for Christ'. The largest and most conservative of the major China missions, the CIM's theological influence can be discerned in bodies as diverse as the Student Volunteer Movement and many of the independent Chinese churches which emerged in the 1920s and 1930s.

Other missionaries adapted their theologies more directly to Chinese cultural, philosophical and religious traditions. The Scottish nonconformist James Legge (1815–97) collaborated extensively with several Chinese colleagues to adapt Ricci's accommodation with Confucianism. Legge's translation of the Chinese canon into English introduced a Christian interpretation of Confucian 'scriptures' in a bid to represent their inherent compatibility with Christian doctrine. For the prominent Welsh Baptist missionary Timothy Richard (1839–1919), the experience of famine relief expeditions in Shandong and Shanxi provinces led him to emphasize the wider welfare of the

Chinese people in addition to their spiritual redemption. Richard developed an idiosyncratic appreciation for the central doctrines and principles of Mahayana Buddhism, hoping that by assimilating the 'worthy' (cf. Matt. 10.11) among China's religious traditions, the Christianization of China would be made possible. A specific 'mission to Buddhists' was developed by the Norwegian Lutheran missionary Karl Reichelt (1877-1952). Reichelt went so far as to adopt Buddhist imagery, adapt Buddhist ritual and liturgy, and build a massive Christian retreat centre in the shape of a Buddhist monastery.

A widespread crisis of confidence affected missionary theologies in China during the later 1920s and 1930s, partly owing to the perceived failure and increased divisions within the missionary movement itself, along with growing nationalist opposition. Longstanding concerns to create a self-sustaining indigenous church became much more urgent. Radical voices such as that of the Anglican Roland Allen (1868-1947) questioned the role of the missionaries in delaying decentralization and imposing a foreign ecclesiology and pneumatology on indigenous churches. Many missionaries came to see their eventual expulsion by the Chinese Communists as the judgement of God: 'our mandate had been withdrawn; the time for missions as we had known them had passed; the end of the missionary era was the will of God' (Oldham, 1955: 424).

 ## Protestant Chinese Christian theologies

> The Chinese indigenization of Protestant Christian theology was a complex process, as early Chinese converts were often discouraged from adapting the theologies which they had been taught (often as young students) by foreign missionaries, or were unwilling to do so.

Nevertheless, even the process of translation and proclamation led to the development of indigenous expressions which became more pronounced in the decades leading up to 1949. Best known among the first generation of Protestant Christians are the southerners Liang Fa (1789-1855) and Ho Tsun Sheen (1818-71). Liang was baptized and trained by the Scottish nonconformist William Milne, before being ordained by Robert Morrison. Liang in turn baptized his wife, and from 1819 began writing tracts, biographical pamphlets, a collection of prayers, and brief introductions to Christian texts and teachings. His most sustained work, entitled *Good Words for Admonishing the Age*, was designed to show that Confucian ethical self-cultivation could only be reached through moral repentance. Ho was a pastor and a close collaborator with James Legge. He is known particularly for his pastoral letters, and is widely credited with the foundation of the first indigenous church in Hong Kong.

The chief exception to the rule of experimentation with the missionary message came with the 'God Worshippers' movement which emerged under the Hakka junior scholar Hong Xiuquan (1813-64). Through reading Liang's tracts, Hong interpreted a series of visions he had had as a sign that he was the younger brother of Jesus Christ, and that it was his mission to rid the world of the Manchu emperors, regarded by many as demons. After instruction by the maverick Baptist missionary Issachar J. Roberts, Hong was refused baptism, but created his own movement. He imposed a strict moral theocracy based on Mosaic laws and radical social equality resting on the common ownership of property, attacked local 'demon-worship' and proclaimed the Taiping or Kingdom of Heavenly Peace. The 'Taiping Rebellion' spread after incompetent efforts by the local government to suppress the movement, and eventually resulted in the Taiping occupation of Nanjing, which was proclaimed the new Heavenly Capital. A decade later, and at a cost of an estimated 30 million lives, Hong and the Taipings were finally defeated by a combination of Chinese and Western military forces. Hong's idiosyncratic theology has left few permanent traces, though many of those followers who survived drifted into the mainstream, missionary-led churches.

A much more orthodox exponent of theological indigenization was the Manchu ecumenist Cheng Jingyi (1881-1939). Cheng was a gifted student and was invited to Scotland in order to help revise the Chinese New Testament. Following graduation from the Glasgow Bible Training Institute, he was invited as one of three Chinese delegates to the Edinburgh Missionary Conference in 1910. Cheng's seven-minute presentation was one of the highlights of the Conference; he pressed for the immediate indigenization of the Chinese church, arguing that it would be self-supporting and self-governing, that an indigenous church would be easier to unify than ones dependent on foreign denominations and that unity was a core Chinese and Christian goal. Returning to China, Cheng was instrumental in the foundation of the National Christian Council in 1922. The plight of the Chinese church, he argued, was 'not [only] her dependence on the liberality of Christians in other countries. Her dependence upon the thoughts, ideas, institutions and methods of work of others is even more serious.' Cheng's ecumenical vision was never realized in his lifetime, but pointed forward to the creation of a 'post-denominational' church in China during the latter half of the twentieth century.

Cheng's call for a contextualization of the Christian faith was taken up by a generation of academic Chinese theologians, mostly based at the mission-run universities at Beijing, Shanghai and Nanjing. They were faced with a surging nationalist consciousness which stressed national strength and modernization, opposed the Christian 'cultural invasion' and (predominantly) espoused a strongly materialist scientism. In response these theologians proclaimed a Sinicized Christology, emphasizing Christ as a figure for national moral renewal. Jesus' example of self-sacrifice fitted the goals of national salvation, and the social revolutionary implications of his teachings led to a 'practical' Christian emphasis on social reconstruction.

The most prominent Christian scholar of this period was Wu Leichuan (1870–1944), who taught at Beijing's Yenching University between 1924 and 1937. Wu's emphasis on indigenization was particularly marked as editor of *Truth and Life* magazine, leading up to his defining work, *Christianity and Chinese Culture* (published in 1936). His theology reflected the interplay of Confucianism, Christianity and materialism typical of his generation of scholars. Wu was particularly interested in the way in which Confucian teachings could elaborate and develop a universal Christianity, removing its 'unnecessary parts' and revealing the 'true way of Jesus'. This unified 'way' could lead to the transformation of contemporary society into the 'Great Unity' which had become the central ideal of the Confucian reformers.

For another scholar, Wang Zhixin, the Chinese indigenous church could only be built on the 'characteristics and inheritance of the Chinese people'. Therefore Wang stressed the centrality of harmony (*tiaohe*) and filial piety (*xiao*) in developing a Christianity fit for modern China. 'National reconstruction' was the primary concern of Fan Zimei (1866–1939), who expressed the view that Christianity was, in essence, an Eastern religion which emphasized virtue over power, peace over violence and ethical service over materialism. Together with a 'Sinicized Jesus', Wang thought these characteristics would allow for the indigenization of Chinese Christianity.

In the longer term, the most prominent Chinese theologian of this period remains Zhao Zichen (1888–1979). Zhao was born into a Buddhist family, but was educated at Presbyterian and Methodist mission schools and university before studying at Vanderbilt University from 1914 until 1917. Zhao subsequently became Professor of Theology and Dean of the School of Religion at Yenching University, roles he would hold into the 1950s. He was widely recognized in the international ecumenical movement, culminating in his appointment as one of the six presidents at the inaugural meeting of the World Council of Churches in 1948. As early as 1920, Zhao had published his own creed, removing 'unscientific' beliefs in the miraculous or the resurrection of the body. Rather than using the conventional *shangdi* or *shen* to refer to God, he preferred the 'philosophically neutral' term *zhuzai* (ruler/sovereign). Through Jesus, the erasure of sin from every human heart was possible, hence the possibility of social reconstruction. Zhao struggled to unravel the Pauline view of salvation in the light of the Confucian emphasis on virtue and self-cultivation, but increasingly came to equate salvation with sanctification. Unlike many of his contemporaries, Zhao moved away from social action during the 1930s, emphasizing instead divine transcendence, though he added his signature to the 'Christian manifesto' in 1950.

The author of the 'manifesto' was the Cantonese Wu Yaozong (Y. T. Wu, 1893–1979), who represented the most radical contextualization of

Christian theology to Chinese political concerns of the 1940s and 1950s. After seven years as a civil servant, Wu became a leading figure in the Chinese YMCA, punctuated by studies in the USA under Reinhold Niebuhr and John Dewey. His distinctive 'political theology' emerged in the 1930s out of an earlier Christian pacifism; at that time, China was increasingly threatened by Japanese invasion and the country was riven by the Nationalist–Communist struggle. Wu's influential work *No Man Has Seen God* (1943) argued that theistic beliefs could be reconciled with materialism, which 'may be the way God reveals Himself in nature'. Wu wrote that China's national salvation depended on a social revolution which combined love with material reconstruction; only this could correct the pre-eminent problem of social injustice. His increasing desire to 'reach out to those who desire to save the country' was made public in his 1948 article 'The Present-Day Tragedy of Christianity', which deplored the churches for being 'reactionary forces moulded by anachronistic capitalistic society'. He was forced to resign from his positions in the YMCA. In the spring of 1950, following the Communist victory, he helped draft the 'Direction of Endeavour for Chinese Christianity in the Construction of New China' (more widely known as the 'Christian manifesto'), which proclaimed that Christianity 'must learn that it is no longer the sole distributor of the panacea for the pains of the world. On the contrary, God has taken the key to the salvation of mankind and given it to another.'

Very different theological responses to the turmoil of the 1940s may be determined in the writings of some of the leading independent Chinese pastors. A Brethren and Holiness-inspired spirituality led the Fujianese Ni Tuosheng (Watchman Nee, 1903–72) to emphasize a primitive 'Local Church' structure for all of the 'elect' in a given location, which would supplant existing churches. Ni emphasized the 'death of the soul' in favour of a life in the 'spirit'. The rapid growth of his 'Little Flock' in the late 1940s was part of a number of Pentecostal-style movements, drawing on the revivalist preaching of figures like Song Shangjie and Ji Zhiwen. Meanwhile, the independent Beijing pastor Wang Mingdao (1900–91) wrote instead on human depravity and the integrity of the sanctified Christian life, leading him to stress the necessity for separation from liberal missionary influences as well as domestic corruption in preparation for the imminent *parousia*. His steadfast refusal to involve himself in the political factions which surrounded the Sino-Japanese conflict and the Nationalist–Communist struggle left a strong impression on subsequent generations of independent 'house-church' leaders.

Chinese Christian theologians' participation in the increasing globalization of theology was curtailed by the events of the 1950s in much the same way as the foreign missionaries' expulsion prevented further foreign influence. Nevertheless, the continued growth and vitality of the Chinese church revealed the living strengths of indigenous Chinese Christian theology and spirituality.

SUGGESTED QUESTIONS

1 What efforts were taken to make Chinese Christianity indigenous? Do you think that the indigenization of Christianity is important? Why?

2 How was Christianity related to Confucianism in the Chinese context? How has Christianity in your own context related to other religions and philosophies?

3 Write about the Protestant influence on the translation of the Bible into Chinese. Write about the history of Bible translation in your own context, paying attention to the various changes that have taken place over the years.

15
Dalit theology: the 'untouched' touching theology

Peniel Jesudason Rufus Rajkumar

 Abstract

Rajkumar gives a broad overview of the social, economic, political, cultural and religious oppression experienced by the Dalits under the caste system. Pointing out how caste discrimination prevails even within Indian Christianity, he goes on to show the failure of Indian Christian contextual theologies as well as Indian theologies of liberation to represent and address the issues facing Dalit communities and their aspirations for liberation. He then traces the origins of Dalit theology and explains three important features of Dalit theology: its experiential nature, which privileges Dalit experiences of pain or 'pathos'; its anticipatory nature, which anticipates a future free from discrimination and injustice; and its counterintuitive nature, which seeks to move away from and reject traditional dominant methods of engaging in theological reflection in the Indian context.

 Introduction

Dalit theology is a form of liberation theology which addresses the issue of the liberation of Dalit communities from caste-based discrimination. It can be called an 'identity-specific' theology because it deals in particular with Dalit communities.

> The term 'Dalit' is the name by which several communities who were previously known as the 'untouchables' prefer to be known today. This is because the term 'Dalit' captures the spirit of struggle amid persistent brokenness.

The Dalits were marginalized and rendered 'outcastes' by the caste system. The caste system is a pervasive form of hierarchical structuring of Indian society on the basis of notions of purity and pollution. Dating back over 3,000 years, the caste system is the oldest surviving hierarchy in the world.

The caste system

Before we proceed further a brief description of the caste system in India would be appropriate. Two words are used for 'caste' in the Indian context, *varna* and *jati*. *Varna*, which literally means 'colour', refers to a broad division of society into four castes on the basis of occupational functions, namely the *Brahmins* (priests and teachers), *Kshatriyas* (rulers and warriors), *Vaishyas* (traders) and *Shudras* (servants who performed menial jobs). In this fourfold *varna* system Dalits had no place in society. They were literally 'no people' and hence were the 'outcastes'. *Jati*, the other term for caste, refers to common origins or birth and pertains to endogamous groups which enjoy a common regional base. In everyday life, particularly in the villages in India, the concept of caste which operates is *jati* rather than *varna*. Although Dalits fall outside the fourfold *varna*, they find a place in the local *jati* system in the villages as one among the *jati*. The Dalits are nevertheless discriminated against in both the *varna* and the *jati* systems.

The survival of the majority of Dalit communities is characterized by resilience and struggle in the midst of severe oppression.

> Most Dalits face social marginalization, political suppression and economic exploitation. Their religion and culture are considered inferior and their women are frequently the targets of sexual violation. Yet several Dalits have managed to assume positions of academic excellence, high level economic entrepreneurship, political, legal and spiritual leadership, and distinction as artists and sportspeople.

However, for most Dalit communities daily existence is a struggle for dignity and for survival with integrity. An oft-quoted passage from *The Human Rights Watch Report* of 1999 describes the life of the Dalits as follows:

> More than one-sixth of India's population, some 160 million people, live a precarious existence, shunned by much of society because of their rank as untouchables or Dalits – literally meaning 'broken' people – at the bottom of India's caste system. Dalits are discriminated against, denied access to land, forced to work in degrading conditions, and routinely abused at the hands of the police and of higher-caste groups that enjoy the state's protection. In what has been called 'hidden apartheid' entire villages in many Indian states remain completely segregated by caste. National legislations and constitutional protections serve only to mask the social realities of discrimination and violence faced by those living below the 'pollution line'. (Human Rights Watch, 1999: 1, 2)

Though the caste system has its origins in Vedic Hinduism, it would be a mistake to assume that all Dalits are Hindus and that Dalits are discriminated against only within Hinduism. In fact we can find people of Dalit origins in all the major religious traditions in India. Therefore we have Hindu Dalits, Muslim Dalits, Christian Dalits, Buddhist Dalits and Sikh Dalits.

The Indian church, casteism and Dalit Christians

Caste discrimination against Christian Dalits is common within the Indian churches, especially in South India.

> The caste system prevails in Indian Christianity because most Indian Christians are converts from Hinduism and have largely retained their caste identities, especially in places where Christians come from various caste backgrounds.

Therefore, Indian Christianity comprises 'caste Christians' alongside Christians of Dalit origins. On the one hand we have several Christian communities with a dominant caste background who have not relinquished their 'social identity' (i.e. caste) and its associated status, privileges and socially exclusive attitudes despite a change in their 'religious identity', while on the other hand we also have Dalit converts who, having chosen to convert to Christianity mainly to escape from caste discrimination, have encountered stigmatization and discrimination on the basis of caste.

Having said this, it needs to be acknowledged that many Christians from a 'dominant' caste background have renounced caste completely and have married outside caste. There are also many Christians who, despite having Dalit origins, prefer to project a single Christian identity and either reject, hide or actively seek to forget their Dalit identity. The point which needs to be emphasized is that the caste-influenced scenario of Christian conversion is rendered all the more complex because in most instances religious mobility (change of religious affiliation) is accompanied by social rigidity (static caste affiliation). It is caste affiliation which, to a large extent, influences and directs the inter-caste interactions within Christianity, especially in South India where Christians come from a spectrum of caste and 'casteless' groups.

Regarding the discrimination faced by Dalit Christians, Saral P. Chatterjee points out that Christian Dalits are 'twice-alienated'. First, they are discriminated against by non-Dalits on the basis of their Dalit identity, and second, they are also marginalized within the Church (Chatterjee, 1998).

M. E. Prabhakar calls casteism within the Indian church a theological contradiction and a spiritual problem and talks about the fourfold alienation of the Christian Dalits, which involves:

Discrimination from the state when it comes to rendering economic assistance, educational benefits or political representation on the basis of their Christian identity. (This is because the state does not recognise casteism within Christianity on the basis that caste is a peculiarly Hindu phenomenon and therefore considers the category of 'Dalit Christians' as being irrelevant)

Disfavour from fellow Dalits especially when Christian Dalits seek governmental assistance, which is based on the common presumption that Christian Dalits have already been uplifted by missionary patronage

Contemptuous treatment from 'upper-caste' Christians, and

Internal conflicts between Christian Dalits on sub-caste, regional or linguistic basis. (Prabhakar, 1998: 205, 206)

 Indian Christian theology and the Dalits

It is not only in social terms that Dalit Christians are underprivileged and discriminated against within Indian Christianity. Even the theological articulations which have emerged within the Indian context have been largely insensitive and oblivious to Dalit issues.

This neglect of Dalit concerns in Indian Christian theology is understandable because, in a context of colonialism, Indian Christian theologians, most of whom were from dominant caste backgrounds, took upon themselves the task of affirming their 'Indianness'. This Indianness was identified solely in terms of Hindu philosophical concepts, Hindu religious texts and other religious resources which were unrelated to Dalit communities. According to Arvind P. Nirmal this resulted in the perpetuation of Indian Christian theology in the 'Brahminic Tradition' (Nirmal, 1990: 27).

James Massey helps in further illustrating the point regarding the irrelevance of Indian Christian theology to the Dalits:

Looking at a standard textbook on Indian Christian theology, one can say that the roots of the current Indian theological expression are in the experiences of mostly upper caste converts. Well known examples are: Brahmabandhab Upadhyara, from a Bengali Brahman family, Sadhu Sundar Singh from a high caste, wealthy Sikh Panjabi family, Nehemiah Gore, a Marathi Brahman, H.A. Krishna Pillai, a high caste Vaishnavite non-Brahman, Narayan Vaman Tilak, from a Brahman family, A.J. Appasamy, from a high caste Saivite family, P. Chenchiah, son of a prominent upper caste lawyer from Andhra, V. Chakkarai from the Chetty caste, a non-Brahman upper caste in Tamilnadu, and so on.

Now if the above names are deleted from current Indian Christian theology, then there will be nothing left behind. But the point which needs to be noted here is that these thinkers and their experiences and search were very different from that of an average Christian in India, because all of them came either from a high caste or their families were rich. So after they became Christians, their immediate concerns were not the same as thousands of those who became

Christians, who were both poor and belonged to the lower strata of society (mostly Dalits). (Massey, 2001)

While this articulation of contextual theology using the very parochial lens of one's own tradition was an important reason why Dalit concerns were neglected by Indian Christian theologians, this was not the only reason. Dalit issues were also not specifically addressed because the subsequent phases of Indian Christian theology tended to focus on broader agendas. Of these phases two need mention. First, following the International Missionary Conference held at Tambaram Madras in 1938, at which Christianity's triumphalist and exclusivist tendencies were strongly critiqued, Christian theologians were keen to build harmonious relationships between Hinduism and Christianity through exploring commonalities and points of convergence between the two traditions. A group of 'upper caste' thinkers popularly known as the Madras Rethinking Christianity Group dominated the theological arena and sought to develop an authentically indigenous Christianity which enhanced interfaith relationships. This pre-Independence phase of Indian Christian theology was followed by a post-Independence stage which had a strong focus on nation building and sought to interpret salvation in broad terms – as 'humanization' – by identifying liberative elements within Hindu renaissance movements with the liberative activity of Jesus Christ the Risen Lord, the Cosmic Christ who permeates even the world outside Christianity. Amid such important yet broad concerns liberation was usually understood in universalist terms and Dalit concerns were not given specific attention.

> Furthermore, though the liberation motif was present within Indian theologizing due to the influence of liberation theologies which predominantly used analytical tools derived from Marxism, Dalit theologians felt that the Marxist analysis, focusing as it did on a class analysis, was inadequate to address the complexity of caste, as a class analysis could not account for the psychological trauma and the social and cultural stigma that Dalit communities faced due to caste-based discrimination.

Therefore, there was a perceived need for a theology which addressed the social, psychological, cultural, economic and political issues faced by the Dalit communities. This in turn led to the emergence of Dalit theology, which was influenced by the Black theology of the African-Americans, the liberation theology movement of Latin America and the Minjung theology movement of Korea.

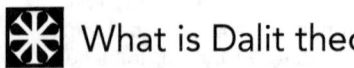 What is Dalit theology?

Defining Dalit theology as a theology from the Dalits, for the Dalits and by the Dalits, Nirmal answers the question 'what is Dalit theology?' in the following manner:

It [Dalit theology] will be based on their own Dalit experiences, their own sufferings, their own aspirations and their own hopes. It will narrate the story of their pathos and their protest against the socio-economic injustices they have been subjected to throughout history. It will anticipate liberation which is meaningful to them. It will represent a radical discontinuity with the classical Indian Christian theology of the Brahminic tradition. (Nirmal, 1998: 219)

> Three important features can therefore be identified in Dalit theology. First, Dalit theology is an experiential theology, based on the 'pathos' experience of the Dalits. Second, it is anticipatory in nature as it anticipates liberation for the Dalits, and therefore is a theology of hope. Third, methodologically Dalit theology is counterintuitive as it intentionally dismantles the Brahminical methodology that forms the basis of Indian Christian theology.

These three features are the important foci of Dalit theology.

Dalit theology as an experiential theology

Dalit theology is based on the Dalit experience of pain or pathos. According to Nirmal, 'It is in and through this pain-pathos that the sufferer knows God. This is because the sufferer in and through his/her pain-pathos knows that God participates in human pain' (Nirmal, 1991: 141).

Nirmal explores this pain-pathos in terms of 'historical Dalit consciousness', which can serve as the essential basis of a Christian Dalit theology as it is both related to the question of Dalit identity and implies recognition of Dalit roots. For Nirmal this historical Dalit consciousness depicts the unparalleled depth of pain and pathos of the Dalits and is the chief factor which authenticates Dalit theology, since for the Dalits their pain or pathos is 'more certain than' any principle, proposition, thought or action. From this epistemological lens of pain and pathos Nirmal explicates how the Deuteronomic creed found in Deuteronomy 26.5–12 can be an appropriate paradigm for Dalit theology. This creed offers space to reflect theologically upon Dalit experience, which in his opinion is far worse than the experiences of the Israelites found in the Deuteronomic creed:

> The historical Dalit consciousness in India depicts even greater and deeper pathos than is found in the deuteronomic creed. My Dalit ancestor did not enjoy the nomadic freedom of the wandering Aramean. As an outcaste, he was also cast out of his/her village. The Dalit bastis (localities) were always and are always on the outskirts of the Indian village. When my Dalit ancestor walked the dusty roads of his village, the Sa Varnas (the caste communities) tied a tree-branch around his waist so that he would not leave any unclean foot-prints and pollute the roads. The Sa Varnas tied an earthen pot around my Dalit ancestor's neck to serve as a spittoon. If ever my Dalit ancestor tried to learn Sanskrit or any sophisticated language, the oppressors gagged him permanently by pouring

> molten lead down his throat. My Dalit mother and sisters were forbidden to wear any blouses and the Sa Varnas feasted their eyes on their bare bosoms. The Sa Varnas denied my Dalit ancestor any access to public wells and reservoirs. They denied him the entry to their temples and places of worship ... My Dalit consciousness therefore, has an unparalleled depth of pathos and misery and it is this historical Dalit consciousness, this Dalit identity that should inform my attempt at a Christian Dalit theology.
> (Nirmal, 1998: 221–2)

From this experience, Dalit theologians have articulated Christologies which project Jesus Christ as the revelation of the God who shares and participates in Dalit suffering. Particularly popular has been Nirmal's image of the Dalit Christ who reveals a Servant God:

> But the God whom Jesus Christ revealed and about whom the prophets of the Old Testament spoke is a Dalit God. He is a servant God – a God who serves. Services to others have always been the privilege of Dalit communities in India ... Their servitude is even more pathetic than that of the Shudras (the lowest caste in the fourfold caste system). Against this background the amazing claim of a Christian Dalit Theology will be that the God of the Dalits, the self-existent, the *Svayambhu* does not create others to do servile work, but does servile work Himself. *Servitude is innate in the God of the Dalits. Servitude is the sva-dharma of the God; and since we the Indian Dalits are this God's people, service has been our lot and our privilege* (emphasis added).
> (Nirmal, 1998: 224)

This focus on suffering and pain and pathos has been critically viewed, however, since such an emphasis runs the risk of romanticizing Dalit pain and pathos and perpetuating passive acceptance of pain and suffering. According to Deenabandhu Manchala, in the twenty-first century context the experiences that should inform Dalit theology are on the one hand the increasing assertiveness of Dalit Christians and on the other the growing openness of non-Dalit Christians and theologians to consider the Dalit issue 'not as an issue that concerns only the Dalits but as one that seriously challenges the credibility of the faith claims of any Christian in India'. In such a context

> there is an urge to expand the horizons of Dalit theology in order to include allies, to expand its ambit and relevance to wider realities, to affirm their identity of protest against an oppressive social system, and to move beyond a victim mindset. Therefore, it is not suffering, Dalit pathos alone but also their experience of struggle to overcome suffering and their determination to risk themselves for the sake of liberation and justice that now needs to be considered as the subject matter of theological reflection.
> (Manchala, 2010: 41)

Anticipation of liberation

> Dalits anticipate liberation through their theologizing by linking Jesus' and God's acts of salvation to their own situation of suffering and their aspiration for a hopeful future in Jesus Christ which is filled with justice and equality.

This anticipation of a future free from caste injustice is what makes Dalit theology a liberation theology. However, two different understandings of liberation emerge in Dalit theology.

First is a material understanding of liberation where liberation is understood in terms of socio-economic betterment. James Massey explains the emergence of this materialistic orientation in the following terms: 'when Dalit theologians speak of Dalit Theology, they are in fact making an affirmation about the need for a theological expression which will help them in their search for daily bread and their struggle to overcome a situation of oppression, poverty, suffering, injustice, illiteracy and denial of human dignity and identity' (Massey, 1997: 63).

Closely related to this understanding is M. E. Prabhakar's understanding of Dalit theology as 'a political theology for social action towards the transformation of injustice, undemocratic and oppressive structures'. For Prabhakar liberation of the Dalits from their socio-economic and political bondage is the point of departure for Dalit theology. 'Dalit theology is *doing theology* in community within the context of the sufferings and struggles of Dalits through dialogue, critical reflection and committed action for building a new life-order' (Prabhakar, 1998: 211).

The second understanding of liberation in Dalit theology is related to the affirmation of Dalit identity. For A. P. Nirmal Dalit theology is a theology of identity which has as its ultimate goal 'the realization of [our] full humanness or conversely, [our] full divinity, the ideal of the *Imago Dei*, the image of God in us' (Nirmal, 1998: 222).

Similarly for Franklyn Balasundaram, 'The goal of Dalit theology is the liberation of the Dalits and their empowerment.' This is possible through affirming 'the good news that God is with them in their struggle, that they are God's children and that they have their own God-given identity and that they are people with worth and dignity'. In Balasundaram's opinion 'the issue of human dignity is more important than the question of economic emancipation' (Balasundaram, 1997: 89-90).

Radical discontinuity with Brahminical foundations

Dalit theology is sometimes known as a counter-theology, though not by all Dalit theologians. This is because Dalit theology in its methodology seeks consciously to reject the Brahminical tradition and attempts to express theology using Dalit traditions and cultural resources. This orientation has challenged Dalit theology to move beyond the understanding of theology as *theologia* (words revealing our understanding of God) to *theo-graphia* (art reflecting our understandings of God), *theo-phoneia* (sound reflecting our understandings of God) and *theo-drama* (performance reflecting our understandings of God). Dalit theology is therefore faith seeking understanding in a plurality of forms. This emphasis on forms of communication which are not confined to texts or words is pertinent because the Dalit communities are not textual communities but predominantly performative and oral communities, who have been systematically denied the privilege of learning languages and acquiring mastery of texts by the caste system. Therefore widening the scope of Dalit 'theologizing' beyond textual or word-centred forms recognizes many Dalits as the agents of theologizing.

As an appropriate methodology for Dalit theology, Abraham Ayrookuzhiel advocates that dominant religious traditions and their dehumanizing potential should be denounced through critical analysis and that counter-cultural models from within the Dalit traditions be lifted up as useful and relevant. There is a need, he asserts, to search 'for roots in terms of theological-ideological resources', which involves 'gathering the positive cultural traditions and values counter to the Brahminic hierarchal values of legitimation of the old power relations' that can be found in the scattered popular traditions of the powerless (Ayrookuzhiel, 1993: 15).

Sathianathan Clarke in his work *Dalits and Christianity: Subaltern Religion and Liberation Theology in India* (1998) has utilized the Dalit symbolic world, especially the Dalit practice of drumming, to understand Jesus Christ as the Drum. In many parts of South India Dalit communities like the Paraiyars in Tamil Nadu, and the Madigas in Andhra Pradesh, have been historically associated with the practice of drumming. In fact for the Paraiyars the *paraimolam* or drum is the basis for their identity. However, the caste communities have ascribed a low and polluted identity to the Paraiyars and other drum-beating castes because drum beating is associated with skinning dead animals to make the drums. This is considered to be a polluted task. Furthermore, Dalit drumming has been predominantly associated with funeral drumming and thus, because of its association with death and spirits, has been viewed as a symbol of pollution.

However, today many Dalit communities take pride in their ancestral art of drum beating and are seeking to recover the dignity and rich culture behind this art. Taking into consideration the importance of the Dalit drum as a signifier of Dalit identity and as a symbolic representation of the Dalits' collective expression of resistance and experience of the divine, Clarke explicates a Christology of the Dalit drum and interprets Christ as drum.

Methodologically Clarke's attempt is useful at various levels. There is a corrective dimension because he corrects the misapprehension and misconception that Dalit religion is demonic by emphasizing the presence of a 'Christic element' in the religious tradition of the Dalits. Moreover, by lifting up the subjugated knowledge of the marginalized this methodology enriches the process and content of Christian theology by systematically recalling and creatively remembering voices that have been silenced throughout history in social discourse. In the process what is set in motion is the redefinition of what constitutes acceptable or appropriate knowledge. This provides a critique of Christian theology's overemphasis on biblicalism, a phenomenon which aids the colonizing and demonizing of the working of God within the oral religions.

Conclusion

In conclusion it needs to be stressed that Dalit theology is quintessentially a justice-seeking and anti-exclusive theology. As a theology of experience and identity it anticipates and inspires the work of Dalits towards socio-economic liberation and seeks to empower Dalits through the affirmation of the subjugated and denigrated Dalit identity. Methodologically it seeks to redress the imbalance in the indigenous resources used to articulate theology. The very process of doing Dalit theology is a political and practical ethic, since it is an act of 'speaking truth to power' from below which seeks to redefine interrelationships between different communities along more egalitarian and mutually affirming lines. Dalit theology is political as it effectively exposes and ruptures the prevailing, sometimes theologically-sustained, hegemony and subverts the political dividends of theology to serve the oppressed and challenge the oppressors. It has facilitated the emergence of new agents of and themes for theologizing, and inherent in this process have been the liberative processes of *de-centering* of the power to theologize and *ideological dismantling* of those theological themes which have the potential to obfuscate injustice and oppression. In short it can be said that Dalit theology is both *theological reflection* and *theo-political action* shaped, sustained and directed by the vision of the divine reign of justice, equality and peace, and is a theology which affirms the fullness of life for all.

 SUGGESTED QUESTIONS

1 Who are the Dalit communities? How are they discriminated against in the Church and wider society?

2 What are the reasons for the emergence of Dalit theology?

3 How do Dalit theologians conceive of liberation? Are their ideas similar to the way in which theologians in your context have thought about liberation?

4 Compare the main features of Dalit theology with any other form of liberation theology which has emerged in your own context.

Glossary

ambivalence the characteristic of not being clearly definable; resisting neat categorizations

bhakti in Hinduism, a path to salvation involving devotion to one particular deity

capitalism a profit-oriented economic system in which the trade and industry of a country are controlled by private powers and not by the state

charismatic derived from Charism (divinely given gifts) and charisma (a leader's ability to inspire), a term referring to the tendency of religious groups towards seeking, developing and exercising the divine gifts (for example within Christianity the 'gifts of the Spirit' like speaking in tongues and prophesying) and/or centred around a charismatic leader

eco-feminism form of analysis which sees both women and nature as being the victims of patriarchal oppression

endogamy the custom of marrying only within a given community

essentialism the view that any entity has a true underlying nature shared by all entities of the same kind

Eurocentric having Europe as its centre

henotheism a doctrine, situated between polytheism and monotheism, involving belief in the existence of more than one god, but with only one supreme god

hermeneutics the science of interpretation, used especially of scriptural exegesis

homogenization the imposition of uniformity

hybridity primarily meaning mixture, a concept used by postcolonial critics to refer, in contexts of colonization, to the collision between the colonized and the colonizer in ways leading to new and complex identities as well as new forms of knowledge which problematized notions of authority and purity

inculturation as used in Christianity, refers to the way Christian doctrine is presented to non-Christian cultures and to the influence of those cultures on the doctrine

indigenization to bring under or subject to indigenous culture or influence

Marxist orientated in thinking towards Marxism, a political and economic theory propounded by Karl Marx which adopts a class perspective in social, political and economic analysis. It assumes that class conflict between the bourgeois and the proletariat is the major influence behind historical change

Glossary

Minjung in Korean theology, those who are oppressed politically, exploited economically, marginalized sociologically, despised culturally and condemned religiously

othered those who are constructed as deviant and out of bounds and thus excluded from participation in the dominant society

oxymoron figure of speech in which terms seemingly contradictory to each other appear together

postcolonialism critical analysis and evaluation of the continuing cultural impact of colonialism

Prajāpati the Vedic creator-god, whose name literally means 'Lord of the beings and Lord of the creatures'

Saivite a follower of Saivism, a tradition within Hinduism that is centred around the God Siva

subaltern in the postcolonial context, anyone who suffers oppression by dominant and powerful groups

systematization to arrange according to an organized system

Vaishnavite a follower of Vaishnavism, a tradition within Hinduism that is centred around the God Vishnu

References and further reading

Abhishiktananda, Swami. *Hindu-Christian Meeting Point: Within the Cave of the Heart.* Bombay: The Institute of Indian Culture, 1969.

Anderson, Allan. *An Introduction to Pentecostalism.* Cambridge: Cambridge University Press, 2004.

Ashcroft, Bill, Griffiths, Gareth and Tiffin, Helen. *The Empire Writes Back: Theory and Practice in Post-Colonial Literatures.* London: Routledge, 1995.

Asian Conference of Third World Theologians, 'Asia's Struggle for Full Humanity: Toward a Relevant Theology', in Douglas J. Elwood (ed.), *Asian Christian Theology: Emerging Themes* (Philadelphia: The Westminster Press, 1980), pp. 101–9.

Association for Theological Education in South East Asia, 'Guidelines for Doing Theologies in Asia', in *International Bulletin of Missionary Research*, vol. 32, no. 2 (April 2008), pp. 77–80.

Ayrookuzhiel, Abraham. 'Dalit Theology: A Movement of Counter-Culture', in James Massey (ed.), *Indigenous People: Dalits, Dalit Issues in Today's Theological Debate* (Delhi: ISPCK, 1998), pp. 250–66.

Ayrookuzhiel, Abraham. 'Religious Legitimations and Delegitimations of Social Relations of Power (Of Caste): The Case of Dalits in Historical Perspective', in *Religion and Society*, vol. 40, no. 4 (December 1993), pp. 3–15.

Azariah, Masilamani. *The Unchristian Side of the Indian Church.* Bangalore: Dalit Sahitya Academy, 1989.

Baago, Kaj. *Pioneers of Indigenous Christianity.* Madras: Christian Literature Society, 1969.

Balasundaram, Franklyn. 'Dalit Struggle and its Implications for Theological Education', in *Bangalore Theological Forum*, vol. 29, nos 3 and 4 (September and December 1997), pp. 69–91.

Balasuriya, Tissa. *Planetary Theology.* Maryknoll, NY: Orbis, 1984.

Banerjea, K. M. *The Arian Witness. Supplementary Essays.* London: Thacker Spink & Co., 1880.

Banerjea, K. M. *The Relation Between Christianity and Hinduism.* Calcutta: Oxford Mission Press, 1881.

Bays, D. *Christianity in China: From the Eighteenth Century to the Present*. Stanford, CA: Stanford University Press, 1996.

Bergunder, Michael. *The South Indian Pentecostal Movement in the Twentieth Century*. Grand Rapids, MI: Wm B. Eerdmans, 2008.

Bhabha, Homi K. *The Location of Culture*. London: Routledge, 1994.

Bong, Sharon A. 'An Asian Postcolonial and Feminist Methodology: Ethics as a Recognition of Limits', in Ursula King and Tina Beattie (eds), *Gender, Religion and Diversity: Cross-Cultural Perspectives* (London and New York: Continuum, 2004), pp. 238-49.

Bong, Sharon A. 'Bodies that Suffer, Resist and Heal', in *Believing with Body and Soul* (Aachen: Institute of Missiology [Desk of Women's Studies in Religion and Feminist Theologies], 2004), pp. 14-15.

Bong, Sharon A. 'Suffering, Resisting, Healing: An Asian View of the Body'. In Janet Martin Soskice and Diana Lipton (eds), *Feminism and Theology* (Oxford: Oxford University Press, 2003), pp. 356-64.

Boyd, R. H. S. *Kristadvaita: A Theology for India*. Madras: Christian Literature Society, 1977.

Boyd, Robin. *Introduction to Indian Christian Theology*. Madras: Christian Literature Society, 1975.

Brock, Rita Narasimha, Jung Ha Kim, Kwok Pui-lan, Seung Ai Yang (eds). *Off the Menu: Asian and Asian North American Women's Religion and Theology*. Louisville, KY: Westminster John Knox, 2007.

Burgess, S. M. (ed.). *Encyclopedia of Pentecostal and Charismatic Christianity*. New York: Routledge, 2006.

Carr, Dhyanchand. *Community of Communities*. Tiruvalla: CSS, 2002.

Chatterjee, Saral P. 'Why Dalit Theology?', in James Massey (ed.), *Indigenous People: Dalits, Dalit Issues in Today's Theological Debate* (Delhi: ISPCK, 1998), pp. 179-200.

Chatterji, Saral K. 'Some Ingredients of a Theology of the People', *Religion and Society*, vol. 27 (1980), pp. 3-28.

Chia, Edmund (ed.). *Dialogue? Resource Manual for Catholics in Asia*. Bangkok: FABC-OEIA, 2001.

Childs, Peter and Williams, R. J. Patrick. *An Introduction to Post-Colonial Theory*. London: Prentice Hall, 1997.

Ching, Leo. 'Yellow Skin, White Masks: Race, Class and Identification on Japanese Colonial Discourse', in Kuan Ksing Chen (ed.), *Trajectories: Inter-Asia Cultural Studies* (London: Routledge, 1988), pp. 65-86.

Chung Hyun Kyung. *Struggle to be the Sun Again: Introducing Asian Women's Theology*. Maryknoll, NY: Orbis, 1990.

Clarke, Sathianathan. *Dalits and Christianity: Subaltern Religion and Liberation Theology in India*. New Delhi: Oxford University Press, 1998.

Commission on Theological Concerns of the Christian Conference of Asia (ed.). *Minjung Theology: People as the Subjects of History*. Maryknoll, NY: Orbis, 1983.

Congregation of Our Lady of Charity of the Good Shepherd (SOLC), <www.buonpastoreint.org>, accessed 18 April 2010.

Constable, Nicole. *Maid to Order in Hong Kong*. Ithaca, NY: Cornell University Press, 1997.

Coulson, Gail V., Herlinger, Christopher, and Anders, Camille S. *The Enduring Church: Christians in China and Hong Kong*. New York: Friendship Press, 1996.

Cox, Harvey. *Fire from Heaven: The Rise of Pentecostal Spirituality and the Reshaping of Religion in the Twenty-first Century*. Reading, MA: Addison-Wesley, 1995.

Cruz, Gemma Tulud. *An Intercultural Theology of Migration: Pilgrims in the Wilderness*. Leiden: Brill, 2010.

Devasahayam, V. (ed.). *Dalits and Women: Quest for Humanity*. Madras: GLTCRI, 1992.

Devasahayam, V. *Doing Dalit Theology in Biblical Key*. Delhi/Madras: ISPCK/GLTCRI, 1997.

Dietrich, Gabriele. 'People's Movements, the Strength of Wisdom and the Twisted Path of Civilization', in Fernando Segovia (ed.), *Toward a New Heaven and a New Earth* (Maryknoll, NY: Orbis, 2003), pp. 407–21.

Eidger, Max. 'Indigenous People – Spirituality and Peace'. Concept paper presented at Asia Pacific Alliance of YMCAs and Interfaith Cooperation Forum, 19–24 October 2007.

England, John C., Kuttianimattahil, Jose, Mansford, John, Quintos, Lily A., Kwang-Sun, David Suh, and Wickeri, Janice (eds). *Asian Christian Theologies: A Research Guide to Authors, Movements, Sources*, volumes 1–3. Maryknoll, NY: Orbis, 2004.

Evers, Georg. *The Churches in Asia*. Delhi: ISPCK, 2005.

Fabella, Virginia and Sugirtharajah, R. S. (eds). *Dictionary of Third World Theologies*. Maryknoll, NY: Orbis, 2000.

Fanon, Frantz. *The Wretched of the Earth*. Harmondsworth: Penguin [1961], 1990.

First Plenary Assembly of the Federation of Asian Bishops' Conferences (FABC), 'Evangelization in Modern Day Asia', in Rosales, Gaudencio and Arévalo, C. G. (eds), *For All the People of Asia: Federation of Asian Bishops' Conferences Documents from 1970 to 1991*, vol. 1 (Quezon City: Claretian, 1997), p. 14.

Fogarty, Philippa. 'Recognition at last for Japan's Ainu', BBC News, <http://news.bbc.co.uk/2/hi/asia-pacific/7437244.stm> (6 June 2008).

Grafe, Hugald. *History of Christianity in India Vol IV, Part 2: Tamilnadu in the Nineteenth and Twentieth Centuries*. Bangalore: Church History Association of India, 1990.

Gutiérrez, Gustavo. *An Asian Theology of Liberation*. London: SCM Press, 1974.

Hall, Stuart. *Encoding and Decoding in the Television Discourse*. Birmingham: Centre for Cultural Studies, 1973.

Hollenweger, Walter J. *Pentecostalism: Origins and Developments Worldwide*. Massachusetts: Hendrickson, 1997.

Human Rights Watch. *Broken People: Caste Violence Against India's 'Untouchables'*. York: Human Rights Watch, 1999.

Ilaiah, Kancha. *Buffalo Nationalism: A Critique of Spiritual Fascism*. Kolkata: Samya, 2004.

Isasi-Diaz, Ada Maria. *En la lucha (In The Struggle): Elaborating a mujerista theology*. Minneapolis: Fortress Press, 1993.

Jathanna, O. V. *The Decisiveness of Christ-Event and the Universality of Christianity in a World of Religious Plurality with Special Reference to Hendrik Kraemer and Alfred George Hogg as well as to William Ernest Hocking and Pandepeddi Chenchiah*. Bern: Peter Lang, 1981.

Jathanna, O. V. 'Indian Christian Theology: Methodological Reflection', *Bangalore Theological Forum*, vol. 18, nos 2–3 (1986).

Joseph, M. P. 'Introduction: Searching Beyond Galilee', in Huang Poho, *From Galilee to Tainan: Towards a Theology of Chhutpthau-thin* (ATESEA Occasional Paper No. 15) (Tainan: ATESEA, n.d.), pp. 5–18.

Joy, C. I. David. *Christology Re-visited: Profiles and Prospects*. Bangalore: ATC, 2007.

Kakuzo, Okakura. *The Ideals of the East*. London: John Murray, 1903.

Kappen, Sebastian. *Jesus and Freedom*. Maryknoll, NY: Orbis, 1977.

Kappen, Sebastian. *Towards a Holistic Cultural Paradigm*. Tiruvalla: CSS, 2003.

Kay, William K. and Dyer, Anne E. (eds). *Pentecostal and Charismatic Studies*. London: SCM Press, 2004.

Kim, Sebastian C. H. (ed.). *Christian Theology in Asia*. Cambridge: Cambridge University Press, 2008.

Kim, Yong-bock. 'Historical Transformation, People's Movement and Messianic Koinonia'. PhD dissertation, Princeton Theological Seminary, 1976.

Kolenchery, Anthony. 'South Indian Contribution to Subaltern Alternative Theologies', *ITS*, vol. 40 (2003), pp. 125–41.

Koyama, Kosuke. *Waterbuffalo Theology*. Maryknoll, NY: Orbis, 1974.

Koyama, Kosuke. 'We had Rice with Jesus', in Jae Shik Oh and John C. England (eds), *Theology in Action* (EACC, 1972), pp. 19–32.

Kuriakose, M. K. *History of Christianity in India: Source Materials*. Madras: Christian Literature Society, 1982.

Kwok Nai Wang, *A Church in Transition*. Hong Kong: Hong Kong Christian Institute, 1997.

Kwok Pui-lan. *Discovering the Bible in the Non-Biblical World*. Maryknoll, NY: Orbis, 1995.

Kwok Pui-lan. *Introducing Asian Feminist Theology*. Cleveland, OH: Pilgrim Press, 2000.

Kwok Pui-lan. *Postcolonial Imagination and Feminist Theology*. Louisville, KY: Westminster John Knox, 2005.

LaRue, C. J. 'The Shape of Coloured Preaching in the 21st Century', in *Masihi Sevak: Journal of Christian Ministry*, vol. 34, no. 2 (August 2009), pp. 18–33.

Latourette, Kenneth Scott. *A History of Christianity*. London: Harper & Row, 1953.

Lee, Archie C. C. 'Cross-textual Hermeneutics and Identity in Multi-scriptural Asia', in Sebastian C. H. Kim (ed.), *Christian Theology in Asia* (Cambridge: Cambridge University Press, 2008), pp. 179–204.

Lee, Jung-Young (ed.). *An Emerging Theology in World Perspective: Commentary on Korean Minjung Theology*. Mystic, CT: Twenty-third Publications, 1988.

Lee, Young-hoon. *The Holy Spirit Movement in Korea: Its Historical and Theological Development*. Oxford: Regnum, 2009.

Lewis, Nantawan Boonprasat. 'On Naming Justice: The Spiritual and Political Connection in Violence against Asian Immigrant Women', in Fernando

Segovia (ed.), *Toward a New Heaven and a New Earth: Essays in Honor of Elisabeth Schüssler Fiorenza* (Maryknoll, NY: Orbis, 2003), pp. 473–86.

Longchar, Wati. 'An Emerging Tribal/Indigenous Theology: Prospect for Doing Asian Theology', in *The Journal for Theologies and Cultures in Asia*, vol. 1 (February 2002), pp. 3–16.

Longchar, Wati. *The Traditional Tribal Worldview and Modernity*. Jorhat, Assam: Eastern Theological College, 1995.

Longchar, Wati (ed.). *The Tribal Worldview and Ecology*. Jorhat, Assam: Eastern Theological College, 1998.

Mananzan, Mary John. 'Emerging Alternatives to Globalization and Transformative Action: Philippine-Asia-Pacific Experience', in *Voices from the Third World*, vol. 21, no. 2 (December 1998), pp. 119–33.

Mananzan, Mary John. 'Reconciliation and the Gender Issue', in *Voices from the Third World*, vol. 21, no. 2 (December 1998), pp. 9–18.

Mananzan, Mary John. *Woman, Religion and Spirituality in Asia*. Manila: Anvil and Institute of Women's Studies, 2004.

Manchala, Deenabandhu. 'Expanding the Ambit: Dalit Theological Contribution to Ecumenical Social Thought', in Sathianathan Clarke, Deenabandhu Manchala and Philip Vinod Peacock (eds), *Dalit Theology in the Twenty-First Century: Discordant Voices Discerning Pathways* (New Delhi: Oxford University Press, 2010), pp. 38–54.

Manickam, T. M. *Dharma According to Manu and Moses*. Bangalore: Dharmaram Publications, 1977.

Martin, David. *Pentecostalism: The World Their Parish*. Oxford: Blackwell, 2002.

Massey, James. *Down Trodden: The Struggle of India's Dalits for Identity, Solidarity and Liberation*. Geneva: World Council of Churches, 1997.

Massey, James. 'Historical Roots', in *Indigenous People: Dalits, Dalit Issues in Today's Theological Debate* (Delhi: ISPCK, 1994), pp. 159–64.

Massey, James. 'Need of a Dalit Theology', *CTC Bulletin*, <http://www.cca.org.hk/resources/ctc/ctc01-04/ctc0104i.htm> (2001).

Massey, James. 'The Role of the Churches in the Whole Dalit Issue', in *Religion and Society*, vol. 41, no. 1 (March 1994), pp. 44–50.

Miller, Donald E. and Yamamori, Tetsunao. *Global Pentecostalism: The New Face of Christian Social Engagement*. Berkeley, CA: University of California Press, 2007.

Minh-ha, Trinh T. *When the Moon Waxes Red: Representation, Gender and Cultural Politics*. London: Routledge, 1991.

Mongia, Padmini. *Contemporary Postcolonial Theory: A Reader*. London: Hodder Arnold, 1996.

Moon, Hee-Suk, 'Jesus Christ, the Crucified Son of Man', <http://warc.ch/where/22gc/bible/03.html>, accessed 16 June 2010.

Moore-Gilbert, B. J. *Postcolonial Theory: Contexts, Practices, Politics*. London: Verso, 1997.

Mundadan, A. M. *History of Christianity in India: From the Beginning up to the Middle of the Sixteenth Century*. TPL: Bangalore, 1984.

Neill, Stephen. 'The Church of India, Burma and Ceylon', in John William Charles Ward (ed.), *The Anglican Communion: A Survey* (Oxford: Oxford University Press, 1948), p. 68.

Niles, D. Perman. 'The Word of God and the People of Asia', in James T. Butler, Edgar W. Conrad and Ben C. Ollenburger (eds), *Understanding the Word: Essays in Honour of Bernhard W. Anderson* (Sheffield: JSOT, 1985), pp. 281–313.

Nirmal, Arvind. P. 'Doing Theology from a Dalit Perspective', in Nirmal, Arvind P. (ed.), *A Reader in Dalit Theology* (Madras: GLTCRI, 1991), pp. 139–44.

Nirmal, Arvind P. *Heuristic Explorations*. Madras: Christian Literature Society, 1990.

Nirmal, Arvind P. 'Towards a Christian Dalit Theology', in James Massey (ed.), *Indigenous People: Dalits, Dalit Issues in Today's Theological Debate* (Delhi: ISPCK, 1998), pp. 214–30.

Oldham, Joseph Houldsworth, *International Review of Mission*, vol. 44 (1955), p. 424.

Orevillo-Montenegro, Muriel. *The Jesus of Asian Women*. Maryknoll, NY: Orbis, 2006.

Pavey, Stephen Carl. 'The Demography of Christianity in Hong Kong', in 'Envisioning/Embodying Christianity in Hong Kong: Theologies of Power and Crisis'. PhD dissertation, University of Kentucky, 2005.

Phan, Peter C. 'Can we Read Interreligious Texts Interreligiously?' in Tatsiong Benny Liew (ed.), *Postcolonial Interventions: Essays in Honor of R. S. Sugirtharajah* (Sheffield: Sheffield Phoenix Press, 2009), pp. 313–31.

Phan, Peter C. 'Jesus the Christ with an Asian Face', *Theological Studies*, vol. 57 (1996), pp. 399–430.

Philip, T.V. *Krishna Mohan Banerjea: Christian Apologist*. Madras: Christian Literature Society, 1982.

Pieris, Aloysius. *An Asian Theology of Liberation*. Maryknoll, NY: Orbis, 1988.

Pieris, Aloysius. 'Asia's Non-Semitic Religions and the Mission of Local Churches', in *An Asian Theology of Liberation* (Quezon City: Claretians, 1988), pp. 35–50.

Pieris, Aloysius. *Love Meets Wisdom: A Christian Experience of Buddhism*. Maryknoll, NY: Orbis, 1989.

Pieris, Aloysius. 'Two Encounters in My Theological Journey' in R. S. Sugirtharajah (ed.), *Frontiers in Asian Theology: Emerging Trends* (Maryknoll, NY: Orbis, 1994), pp. 141–6.

Pope Paul VI. *Nostra Aetate*, 'Vatican II's Declaration on the Relationship of the Church to Non-Christian Religions', in Walter Abbott (ed.), *The Documents of Vatican II* (New Jersey: New Century, 1966), p. 662.

Pope Paul VI, *On the Ways in which the Church must Carry out its Mission in the Contemporary World* (Vatican City, 6 August 1964), <http://www.vatican.va/holy_father/paul_vi/encyclicals/documents/hf_p-vi_enc_06081964_ecclesiam_en.html>.

Prabhakar, M. E. 'Christology in Dalit Perspective', in V. Devasahayam (ed.), *Frontiers of Dalit Theology* (Madras/Delhi: GLTCRI and ISPCK, 1997), pp. 402–32.

Prabhakar, M. E. 'The Search for a Dalit Theology', in James Massey (ed.), *Indigenous People: Dalits, Dalit Issues in Today's Theological Debate* (Delhi: ISPCK, 1998), pp. 201–13.

Prabhu, Joseph. 'Foreword' in Raimon Panikkar, *The Rhythm of Being*. Maryknoll, NY: Orbis, 2010.

Rajkumar, Peniel. *Dalit Theology and Dalit Liberation: Problems, Paradigms and Possibilities*. Farnham: Ashgate, 2010.

Razu, John Mohan. *Global Capitalism as Hydra*. Delhi: ISPCK, 2006.

Rey Chow, 'Between Colonizers: Hong Kong's Postcolonial Self-writing in the 1990s', *Diaspora: A Journal of Transnational Studies*, vol. 2, no. 2 (1992), pp. 151–70.

Roe, James Moulton. *A History of the British and Foreign Bible Society*. London: British and Foreign Bible Society, 1965.

Said, Edward. *Orientalism*. Harmondsworth: Penguin, [1978], 1985.

Samartha, S. J. *One Christ – Many Religions: Towards a Revised Christology*. Maryknoll, NY: Orbis, 1991.

Scott, James. *Domination and the Arts of Resistance*. New Haven, CT: Yale University Press, 1990.

Segovia, Fernando F., and Tolbert, Mary Ann. *Reading from this Place: Social Location and Biblical Interpretation in the United States*. Minneapolis: Fortress Press, 1995.

Segovia, Fernando F., and Tolbert, Mary Ann. *Reading from this Place*, Vol. II, *Social Location and Biblical Interpretation in Global Perspective*. Minneapolis: Fortress Press, 1995.

Segovia, Fernando F., and Tolbert, Mary Ann. *Teaching the Bible: The Discourse and Politics of Biblical Pedagogy*. Maryknoll, NY: Orbis, 1998.

Sen, Amartya. *The Argumentative Indian: Writings on Indian History, Culture and Identity*. New Delhi: Penguin, 2005.

Shaull, Richard, and Cesar, Waldo. *Pentecostalism and the Future of the Christian Churches*. Grand Rapids, MI: Wm B. Eerdmans, 2000.

Shohat, Ella. 'Notes on "Post-Colonial"', *Society Text*, nos 31/32 (1992), pp. 99–113.

Smith, Carl. *Chinese Christians: Elites, Middlemen, and the Church in Hong Kong*. Hong Kong: Oxford University Press, 1985.

Smith, George. *A Narrative of an Exploratory Visit to Each of the Consular Cities of China and to the Islands of Hong Kong and Chusan, in behalf of the Church Missionary Society, in the Years 1844, 1845, 1846*. London: Hatchard & Son, 1847.

Soares-Prabhu, George. 'Two Mission Commands: In Interpretation of Matthew 28:16–20 in the Light of a Buddhist Text', in *Biblical Interpretation: A Journal of Contemporary Approaches*, vol. 2, no. 3 (1994), pp. 264–82.

Song, C. S. *Jesus, the Crucified People*. New York: Crossroad, 2000.

Spivak, Gayatri Chakravorty. 'Can the Subaltern Speak?', in Cary Nelson and Larry Grossberg (eds), *Marxism and the Interpretation of Culture* (Chicago: University of Illinois Press, 1988), pp. 271–313.

Spivak, Gayatri Chakravorty. 'Displacement and the Discourse of Woman', in Mark Krupnik (ed.), *Displacement: Derrida and After* (Bloomington: Indiana University Press, 1983), pp. 169–95.

Spivak, Gayatri Chakravorty. *In Other Worlds: Essays in Cultural Politics*. London: Methuen, 1987.

Standaert, N., and Tiedemann, R. G. (eds). *Handbook of Christianity in China*, 2 vols, *635–1800* and *1800 to the Present*. Leiden: Brill, 2000, 2009.

Sugirtharajah, R. S. *Asian Biblical Hermeneutics and Postcolonialism: Contesting the Interpretations*. Sheffield: Sheffield Academic Press, 1998.

Sugirtharajah, R. S. 'Introduction', in R. S. Sugirtharajah (ed.), *Frontiers in Asian Christian Theology: Emerging Trends* (Maryknoll, NY: Orbis, 1994), pp. 1–8.

Sugirtharajah, R. S. *Postcolonial Reconfigurations: An Alternate Way of Reading the Bible and Doing Theology*. London: SCM Press, 2003.

Suh, David Kwang-sun. 'A Biographical Sketch of an Asian Theological Consultation', in Christian Conference of Asia: Commission on Theological Concerns, *Minjung Theology: People as the Subjects of History* (New York: Orbis Books, 1983), pp. 15–37.

Sundkler, Bengst. *Church of South India: The Movement towards Union 1900/1947*. London: USCL, 1965.

Sunquist, Scott W. (ed.). *A Dictionary of Asian Christianity*. Grand Rapids, MI: Wm B. Eerdmans, 2001.

Suurmond, Jean-Jacques. *Word and Spirit at Play: Towards a Charismatic Theology*. Grand Rapids, MI: Wm B. Eerdmans, 1994.

Swidler, Leonard. *After the Absolute: The Dialogical Future of Religious Reflection*. Minneapolis: Fortress, 1990.

Tagore, Rabindranath. *Gora*. Madras: Macmillan, [1924], 1989.

Thangasamy, D. A. *The Theology of Chenchiah with Selections from his Writings*. Bangalore: The Christian Institute for the Study of Religion and Society and The Literature Department of the National Council of YMCAs in India, 1966.

Thomas, M. M. *Man and the Universe of Faiths*. Madras: Christian Literature Society, 1974.

Tinker, George. 'American Indian and the Art of the Land', in *Voices From the Third World*, vol. 14, no. 2 (1981), pp. 170–93.

Tinker, George. 'Spirituality and Native American Personhood: Sovereignty and Solidarity', in K. Abraham and B. Mbuy (eds.), *Spirituality of the Third World* (Maryknoll, NY: Orbis, 1994), pp. 119–32.

Uhalley, Stephen, Jr, and Xiaoxin Wu (eds). *China and Christianity: Burdened Past, Hopeful Future*. Armonk, NY: M. E. Sharpe, 2001.

Wells, Kenneth M. (ed.). *South Korea's Minjung Movement: The Culture and Politics of Dissidence*. Honolulu: University of Hawaii Press, 1995.

Wilfred, Felix. 'Introduction: The Art of Negotiating the Frontiers', *Concilium*, vol. 2 (1999), pp. vii–xiii.

Williams, Delores. *Sisters in the Wilderness: The Challenge of Womanist God-Talk*. Maryknoll, NY: Orbis, 1993.

Williams, Patrick and Chrisman, Laura. *Colonial Discourse and Post-Colonial Theory: A Reader*. New York, London: Harvester Wheatsheaf, 1993.

Wilson, Everett. 'They Crossed the Red Sea, Didn't They?' in Marray Dempster et al. (eds), *The Globalization of Pentecostalism* (Oxford: Regnum, 1999), p. 106.

Wing-Hung Lam. *Chinese Theology in Construction*. Pasadena: W. Carey Library, 1983.

Wong, Wai-Ching Angela. *'The Poor Woman': A Criticial Analysis of Asian Theology and Contemporary Chinese Fiction by Women*. New York: Peter Lang, 2002.

Wong, Wai-Ching Angela. 'Negotiating Gender Identity: Postcolonialism and Christianity in Hong Kong', in Eliza Lee (ed.), *Gender and Change in Hong Kong: Globalization, Postcolonialism and Chinese Patriarchy* (Vancouver: British Columbia University Press, 2004), pp. 151–76.

Yeung, I. Kwok-keung. 'Representing "Asia" in the Globalizing World: Revisiting the Idea of Doing Theology with Asian Cultural Resources', in *Journal of Theologies and Cultures in Asia*, vol. 1 (February 2002), pp. 135–56.

Yogachandra, Nat. *Beauty, Bureaucrats, and Breaking the Silence: The Status of Women in Asia*. New York: Global Arts Group, 2003.

Journals

Asia Journal of Pentecostal Studies
Evangelical Review of Theology
International Review of Mission
Journal of Pentecostal Theology
Pneuma

Index

Abhishiktananda, Swami 50
Adivasis *see* Tribal theology
Ahn Byung-Mu 112
Ainu, the 86
Allen, Roland 127
Amaladass, Anand 50
Anglicanism, and biblical interpretation 50-1
Appasamy, A. J. 51
Aristotle 8
Asia Pacific Alliance of YMCAs 92
Asian Christian theology: advent of 18-19; method and task 4-6; multi-scriptural 10-12
Asian Conference of Third World Theologians 75-6
Assemblies of God 100, 101
Ayrookuzhiel, Abraham 140

Balao, James 84
Balasundaram, Franklyn 139
Balasuriya, Tissa 6
Banerjea, Krishna Mohun 25, 49-50, 116-18, 122
baptism 101, 103
Baptists of the New Life Mission 105
Barth, Karl 121
Bhabha, Homi K. 42, 43, 62
Bible Bhashyam 51
Bible, the 32; affirmation of life 94-5; as Asian scripture 37; and Dalits 11; and local languages 85-6; translation into Chinese 126
biblical interpretation 10-12; Anglicist approach 50-1; historical-critical approach 33, 50; Nativistic approach 51; Orientalist approach 49-50; postcolonial criticism 52-5; text-alone approach 33; text-context approach 33-4; and women's theology 27
biblical theology 50-1
biblicalism 140
Bong, Sharon A. 43
Boyd, R. H. S. 50
Boyd, Robin 119
Brahma Vakya *Aham Brahmasmi* 121-2
'Brahminic Tradition' 135
Buddha 8
Buddhism 14, 18, 124, 125, 127

Carr, Dhyanchand 70-1
caste system 132-4
Catholic theologies in China 124-5
Chakkarai, Vengal 118
Chatterjee Saral P. 134
Chatterji, Saral K. 69-70
Chenchiah, Pandipeddi 118, 119-22
Cheng Jingyi 128
Children of God 122
China Inland Mission (CIM) 126
Chinese theology: Jesus Christ in 125, 128-9
Ching, Leo 6
Chow, Rey 61
'Christian Faith Statement in View of the Present Social and Political Changes in Hong Kong, A' 60
Christian manifesto (1950) 129-30
Christian Tabernacle 100
Christology: Asian 65-8; Chenchiah 119; Dalit 70; feminist 68; liberation 68-9, 70; postcolonial 71; Sinicized 128-9; subaltern 69-71

Chung Hua Sheng Kung Hui 58
Chung Hyun Kyung 10, 26, 27, 43
Church of South India 67
Clarke, Sathianathan 140
colonial pietistic theologies 28
colonialism 6, 17, 42, 43; and culture critique 25-6; Hong Kong 57-9; and indigenous theology 90; and poverty 27; resistance to 24-6
Confucian-Christian dialogue 125
Confucianism 14, 124, 125, 126, 129
Cordillera People's Alliance (CPA) 84
creation: God in 94; and indigenous theology 90, 91-2, 93-5; integrity of, and liberation 94-5; Jesus Christ in 120; plurality of 95-6; revelation as 120
cross-textual hermeneutics: con/textuality and 34-6; in context 31-2; and the reader 36, 37
culture 80-1; and Pentecostalism 104; and reason 26

Dalit theology 9, 29-30, 137-40, 141; Christ-ology 70; a counter-theology 139-40; definition of 136-7, 141
Dalits 84, 86; and the Bible 11; within caste system 133; discriminated against 134-5; drumming 140; and Indian Christian theology 135-6; suffering of, and

155

Index

Jesus Christ 137-8; use of term 132
Daoism 124
'Declaration of Religious Freedom, The' 60
dehumanization, resistance to 29
Delotavo, Allan J. 28
Deuteronomic creed 137-8
Devadas, Mungamuri 51
Dewey, John 130
dialogical model of theology 20-1, 89
Dietrich, Gabriele 79
Direction of Endeavour for Chinese Christianity in the Construction of New China 129-30
'Double Baptism' xv
Dudi of Basra, Bishop 66
Duff, Alexander 50

Ecclesia of Women in Asia 44
Ecclesiam Suam 19
eco-feminism 28
Ecumenical Association of Third World Theologians (EATWOT) 78
ecumenism 105
essentialism 26
evangelism, Hong Kong 57-9
evangelization, task of 20
exodus 95
exorcism 102, 103

Fabella, Virginia 10
Fanon, Frantz 53
Federation of Asian Bishops' Conferences (FABC) 20
feminist theology 9, 10, 26-7, 77, 78-9, 81; Christology 68; and globalization 45-6, 78-9; postcolonial studies 42-6; suffering of Jesus Christ 43
Fogarty, Philippa 86
furrow metaphor xiii-xiv, xv

Gama, Vasco da 66
Gell, Bishop 66-7
George V, King 49
gifts of the Spirit 102
globalization 9, 28, 44, 52, 76, 77, 78-9; and feminist theology 45-6, 78-9; and indigenous people 84-5; and indigenous theology 90
glocalization 45
Gnanadasson, Aruna 28
God: Chinese terms for 126, 129; in the community 80; in creation 94; and indigenous theology 90, 91-2, 93, 94; and liberation 95; pain and pathos 137-8; relationship to Christ and humanity 8; shared 4-5; spaciousness of 7, 8; suffering of 28-9
'God Worshippers' movement 128
Gospel for Asia 105
Great Unity 129
Gregorios, Paul 50
Gutiérrez, Gustavo 23, 24
Gützlaff, Karl 126

Hagar 80
Hall, Stuart 53
Hau Lian Kham 100
'hidden transcripts' strategies 78-9, 81
Hindu-Christian relations 136
Hinduism 116, 118-19; the incarnation in 121; and 'Indianness' 135
Ho Tsun Sheen 127
Hong Kong: 1997 handover 59-61; colonialism 57-9; evangelism 57-9; postcolonialism 56-7, 61-3
Hong Kong Chinese Christian Churches Union 58
Hong Kong Christian Council 58, 60
Hong Kong Church Renewal Movement 59
Hong Xiuquan 128
Horsley, Richard 71
Houtart, Françoise 28
Huang Po Ho 26
Human Rights Watch Report 133

Ilaiah, Kancha 11
incarnation, the 67, 70, 120-2

Indian Christian theology: and the Dalits 135-6; liberation motif 136
indigenous people: ancestral land 86; ecclesial vision 95-6; and globalization 84-5; identity of 83-4, 86; language of 85-6; and missionaries 87, 88, 90, 96; religious rights 85; and the sex trade 87
indigenous theology 87-8; and colonialism 90; and creation 90, 91-2, 93-5; and globalization 90; and God 90, 91-2, 93, 94; and the Jesus movement 91, 94; spiritual connection with earth's family 92-3; stages of 88-90
Intercultural Theology of Migration: Pilgrims in the Wilderness, An (Cruz) 77
Interfaith Cooperation Forum 92
interfaith dialogue: and Asian theology 19-20; forms of 20-2; terms used 14-15; and the West 15-17
International Earth Day 92-3
International Missionary Conference 136
Isasi-Diaz, Ada Maria 80

Jacob, Bishop 67
Jaebul 111-12
Jathanna, O. V. 119
jati 133
Jesuits 125
Jesus Christ 12; in Chinese theology 125, 128-9; as co-sufferer 29; in creation 120; and Dalit suffering 137-8; death as primordial sacrifice 116-18; as the drum 140; gender of 68; interpreter of God and human beings 4-5; and liberation 95; as 'many-breasted woman' 10; and martyrdom 95; as Minjung 112, 113, 114; name of

Index

118; as 'new (hu)Man' 120–1; particularity of 70; in Pentecostalism 104; and the poor 8–10; as *Prajâpati* 116–18, 122; as Priest of *Han* 10; relationship to God and humanity 8; as spiritual mother 118–19; suffering of, and women's bodies 43; transcendence of 121–2; uniqueness of 119–22
Jesus movement 91, 94
Ji Zhiwen 130
John of Monte Corvino 66
John Paul II, Pope 15
Journal of Tribal Studies 86
Jubilee 95
Jun Tae-Il 111

Kagawa, Toyohiko 100
Kakuzo, Okakura 3
Kappen, Sebastian 69
Kingdom of Heavenly Peace 128
Kinukawa, Hisako 44–5
Knitter, Paul 23–4
Kolenchery, Anthony 69
Korean Christian Manifesto 111
Koyama, Kosuke 8
Kraemer, Hendrik 118, 121
Kuster, Volker 67
Kwok Nai Wang 59
Kwok Pui-lan 26, 27, 42, 68

LaRue, C. J. 97
Latourette, Kenneth Scott 67
Legge, James 57, 126, 127
Lewis, Nantawan Boonprasat 81
Liang Fa 127
liberation: and creation 94–5; Dalit theology 138–9, 141; God 95; Indian Christian theology 136; indigenous theology 94–5; and Jesus Christ 95; Minjung theology 112, 113–14
liberation theology 89–90, 113; definition of 24; Palestinian 29; women's 80

'Little Flocks' 100
Longchar, Wati 77, 80

Madras Rethinking Christianity group 118–19, 136
Mahayana Buddhism 127
Mananzan, Mary John 10, 42, 77
Manchala, Deenabandhu 138
Manickam, T. M. 50
Marxism 28, 68–9, 136; and Minjung theology 113
Massey, James 70, 135, 139
materialism 102, 128, 129, 130
militarism 42, 43, 76–7
Milne, William 127
Minjung movement 111–14
Minjung theology 9, 29, 79; and Jesus Christ 112, 113, 114; liberation and justice 112, 113–14; Marxism 113; and self-identity 113–14
miracles 102, 103
missionaries: ideology 31; and indigenous people 87, 88, 90, 96
Moon Hee-Suk 79
Moore, Stephen D. 71
Morrison, Robert 126, 127
Mukti mission, Pune 99
Mundadan, A. M. 66

Nee, Watchman 100
Neill, Stephen 66
Nepalese Christian Fellowship 105
Nestorian Christianity 124–5
Ni Tuosheng 130
Nicolas de Pistoia 66
Niebuhr, Reinhold 130
Niles, D. Perman 34
Nirmal, Arvind P. 70, 135, 136–8, 139
Nostra Aetate 19

Off the Menu: Asian and Asian North American Women's Religion and Theology 46
Oldham, Joseph Houldsworth 127
Orevillo-Montenegro, Muriel 10

Orientalism, and biblical interpretation 49–50
Orr, Edwin 99

Pacific, Asia, and North American Asian Women in Theology and Ministry 46
Panikkar, Raimon 6
Pantaenus 66
Parmalin community 85
patriarchy 44; resistance to 26–7
Paul VI, Pope 19–20
Pentecostalism: cross-society 103–4; and culture 104; definition of 98; doctrines 101–2; ecumenism 105; and ethics 104; Jesus Christ in 104; and need 104; origins of 98–9; personal contact 105; and politics 105; and social engagement 104; and the supernatural 103; worship and church life 106
people's theology 70
Perera, Marlene 45
Phan, Peter 11
philosophical model of theology 88–9
Pieris, Aloysius xv, 9, 17, 23, 28, 77
Pillai, H. A. Krishna 51
planetary theology 6
pluralism, religious 7–8, 16–17
poor, the: and Jesus Christ 8–10; redemptive potential of 28; *see also* poverty
postcolonial studies 40–2; and biblical interpretation 52–5; Christology 71; developments 43–5; feminist theology 42–6; origins 42
postcolonialism: Hong Kong 56–7, 61–3
poverty 75–7; resistance to 27–9; *see also* poor, the
Prabhakar, M. E. 134–5, 139, 141
Prabhu, Joseph 6
prayer 102, 103
Protestant Chinese Christian theologies 127–30

157

Protestant Christian theologies, Chinese indigenization of 128–30
Protestant missionary theologies in China 126–7

Ramabai 99
Razu, John Mohan 28
Reichelt, Karl 127
resurrection 95
revelation, as creation 120
Ricci, Matteo 125, 126
Richard, Timothy 126–7
Ringe, Sharon 71
'rites controversy' in China 125
Roberts, Issachar J. 57, 128
Robertson, Roland 45

Said, Edward W. 42
Samartha, Stanley 8, 17, 18
sanctification 101–2
Sanskrit 49–50, 51
Sapporo Young Men's Christian Association 99
School of Peace, Bangalore 92
Schreiter, Robert J. 67
Schüssler Fiorenza, Elisabeth 71
Scott, James 78
Second Vatican Council (Vatican II) 19
Segovia, Fernando F. 71
Sell, Canon 66–7
Sen, Amartya 9
Shohat, Ella 53
Singh, Sadhu Sundar 51, 99
Smith, Carl 62
Smith, G. 57

Soares-Prabhu, George 54
sobaliba 26
Song, C. S. xiv, 10
Song Shangjie 130
South India United Church 66
Spivak, Gayatri Chakravorty 42
Stanton, Vincent J. 57–8
Student Volunteer Movement 126
Sugirtharajah, R. S. 7–8, 11–12, 26, 42, 67
Suh, David Kwang-sun 29
Suh Nam Dong 112
Sundan 85
Sung, John 100
survival, theology of 79–81
Swidler, Leonard 15

Tagore, Rabindranath 54–5
Taiping 128
Taylor, James Hudson 126
tenants, parable of 53
Thangasamy, D. A. 120, 121–2
Thomas, Apostle 66
Thomas, M. M. 29
Tiananmen Square 60
Tilak, Vaman 51
tlawmngaihna 26
Tolbert, Mary Ann 71
'Translation Method' of theology 88
Tribal theology 9, 11, 84, 86

Uchimira, Kanzo 99–100
UN Millennium Development Goals 76
University of Hong Kong 59

Upadhyay, Brahmabandhab 25

Vandana, Sister 50
varna 133
Vasanji, M. G. 48
Vedic Hinduism 49–50, 134
Vedic theology 116–18
via crucis 75–7

Wang Ming Dao 100, 130
Wang Zhixin 129
Western Christianity in Asia 17–18
Wilfred, Felix 70, 71
Williams, Delores 79–81
Wilson, Everett 98
Women's International War Crimes Tribunal 44
women's theology *see* feminist theology
Wong, Wai Ching Angela 43
World Council of Churches 129
Wu Leichuan 129
Wu Yaozong 129–30

Xavier, Francis 67
Xi Xi 62–3

Yang Tingyun 125
Yeung, Kwok-keung 5
Yogachandra, Nat 77
Yoido Full Gospel Church, South Korea 105
Yongi Church, South Korea 106

Zhao Zichen 129
Zimei, Fan 129

www.ingramcontent.com/pod-product-compliance
Lightning Source LLC
Chambersburg PA
CBHW071204070526
44584CB00019B/2914